Guilford County

County

A Brief History

Guilford County

A Brief History

Alexander R. Stoesen

© 1993 by the
North Carolina Division of Archives and History

ISBN 0-86526-258-6

*For Carol and also for all those Guilfordians,
too numerous to mention,
who have helped make the county what it is today*

Contents

Maps and Illustrations

Foreword

The publication of *Guilford County: A Brief History* marks the thirteenth volume to appear in a series of concise county histories. The Historical Publications Section began publishing the county history series in 1963. Over the years students, teachers, tourists, scholars, and genealogists have come to rely on the county histories for their research needs. The brief histories offer pertinent data, broad surveys, and sound interpretations of people, places, and regions that have enriched North Carolina's diverse heritage.

Alexander R. Stoesen is particularly well suited to write a history of Guilford County. He has taught at Guilford College for a quarter of a century. Moreover, he coauthored with Blackwell P. Robinson a longer history of the county for Guilford's American Revolution Bicentennial Commission, and he has also published a history of Guilford College. Dr. Stoesen received his doctorate in history from the University of North Carolina at Chapel Hill.

In preparing this booklet for publication Dr. Stoesen had the able assistance of Robert M. Topkins, who edited the manuscript, prepared the index, and saw the volume through press. Lisa D. Bailey contributed her proofreading skills, and Sandra T. Hall entered the manuscript on a computer for typesetting.

Jeffrey J. Crow
Historical Publications Administrator

October 1993

Preface

This series of brief county histories has proven "popular with citizens, teachers, schoolchildren, and tourists." A more diversified audience probably could not be found, so the historian is left the quandary of determining how to address "everyone."

Guilford County is the third most populous and the most industrialized county in North Carolina. Having been formed in 1771, it is one of the oldest counties in the state and has a history that moves from primitive settlements to massive industrialization and urbanization. It contains two of the state's largest cities—Greensboro and High Point—each of which has a larger population than seventy of North Carolina's 100 counties. The task of the historian is not made easier by the existence in Guilford of three large governmental units. In many respects the histories of the cities tend to overshadow that of the county, and yet all are part of the same larger political entity. Because of this diversification, Guilford's history is more complex than that of many counties in the state; this fact presents a challenge for historian and reader alike.

The picture presented in this volume is chronological, giving the reader a sense of change over time. Each chapter covers a myriad of topics—important persons and events, government, education, economics, public health, daily life, and transportation. The latter has contributed more to the county's prominence than any other single factor.

Many topics have been omitted, not because they are not of interest but because the historian must be selective. The evolution of the public library system, the rise and demise of hospitals, the churches and the religious life of the people in the nineteenth and twentieth centuries, and details of city-limit expansions and neighborhood developments are but a few such examples.

Frustration will result if this volume is being used as the definitive work on a specific topic, but it is hoped that the work will pique the reader's interest and encourage him or her to delve further. The bibliography merely hints at the possibilities of further reading.

Guilford has been my home through choice for more than twenty-five years. I hope this book helps you to appreciate it as much as I do.

Alexander R. Stoesen
October 1993

I
Origins to 1830

No rivers or other natural boundaries give Guilford County any distinct lines. On maps the county is merely a rectangle; it is 25 miles wide and 26 miles long and is similar in shape to almost half the counties in the United States. Two small rivers—the Haw and the Deep—cut across Guilford's northeast and southwest corners respectively but have never played any significant role in the county's development. The county remained essentially isolated until the 1850s, when railroads gave it access to the outside world.

In the mid-eighteenth century the land that became Guilford County was not easy to reach, and only the most determined settlers were willing to contend with the hardship and anxiety involved in such a journey. But going to that land could be worth the effort. Virtually all of the Siouan-speaking native Americans were gone, victims of warfare and disease, so that the land was uninhabited. The climate was pleasant, and it was probably a more healthful place than the eastern part of North Carolina. Policies implemented by colonial governmental authorities afforded many opportunities for settlers to obtain land in a part of the colony of North Carolina far enough away from the center of British power to satisfy the pursuit of freedom that motivated some settlers. Those settlers sought a land claim, and the area that became Guilford County was desirable and available.

A hardwood forest covered most of the region, providing plentiful material for cabins, outbuildings, and fences. Settlers set about clearing trees almost immediately, then began to plow a soil that has been described in technical terms as mostly Enon-Mecklenburg (49 percent) and Cecil-Madison (29 percent). Those soils are well drained and known to be well suited to agriculture and forestry. The technical language would not have meant much to the early settlers, who probably could have provided the description for themselves. The soil was ideal for the crops they most wanted to raise—corn, flax, and vegetables. Settlers also understood the importance of drainage patterns. Many small streams crossed the countryside; they provided both water and in some places power. A gristmill on a stream was a distinct advantage in an economy that relied almost entirely upon barter. Settlement began in earnest in the mid-1750s, and within about twenty years most of the best land and locations were taken.

What is now Guilford initially was part of Orange County, with its seat at Hillsborough. There the justices of the county court, known as the court of pleas and quarter sessions, met four times a year to try minor cases. The court provided entertainment for people who came to watch the proceedings, mingle, and enjoy the provisions of nearby taverns. In addition to trials, the county court was responsible for county administration. It issued licenses, maintained roads, collected taxes, and decided on the location of mills. Since the justices were not elected but were appointed by the governor and his council, the system had an extraordinary potential for the development of corruption, which became a reality. One of the results of that corruption was the Regulation (1766-1771), which broke out when backcountry farmers rebelled against officials who overcharged them for services and retained a portion of the taxes they collected.

After the War of the Regulation, which culminated in the Battle of Alamance in 1771, North Carolina's colonial legislature, known as the Assembly, created several new counties as a means of achieving greater administrative control over the growing population in the Piedmont. In 1771 the British created Guilford—which then included present-day Rockingham and Randolph counties—from portions of old Orange County and named it for the earl of Guilford, a friend of George III, king of England, and the father of Lord North. The population of the original Guilford County was about 10,000. By 1774 a log courthouse and jail had been erected on the Salisbury road, near the middle of the county. That place was known simply as Guilford Courthouse.

Most of Guilford's early citizens were staunchly religious people, strongly attached to their denominations' practices and beliefs. Among them were members of the religious Society of Friends, commonly known as Quakers, who settled in the western part of the county beginning about 1750. At about the same time, German Lutherans were arriving in the eastern part of the county. The middle and southern parts of Guilford were the destination of Presbyterians and Methodists, some of whom were as strongly pacifist as the Quakers. The early settlers were seekers after good land, which they found and were determined to keep. Quakers, not usually given to exaggeration, named their first settlement New Garden.

After the War of the Regulation the colonial authorities sought to reform and improve local government, but administrative changes probably had little effect on the lives of a population of subsistence farmers, who bartered surpluses for necessities and minor luxuries and made matters of the spirit a major concern in their lives. In most ways Guilford was similar to any other part of central North Carolina. It was quiet, isolated, and with a population so scattered that no town existed.

There was, however, one person who stood out in this place where hopes and ambitions could easily be swamped in the daily struggle for existence. That person was David Caldwell, a Presbyterian minister and educator, who attempted unsuccessfully to be a peacemaker prior to the War of the Regulation. Unable to head off conflict, he worked, again without success, to obtain clemency for the condemned Regulators. Caldwell's main contribution, however, was in the realm of education, for it was his interest in that subject that inaugurated Guilford County's traditional association with education and educational institutions. It began in 1767 when Caldwell opened his famous "log college" on a farm in what is now northwest Greensboro.

Even though Caldwell was then serving as minister for two Presbyterian churches, he saw a need for a school in the wilderness. His log college was the result. The primary goal was education for the ministry, but Caldwell devised a curriculum that added science and mathematics to the classical subjects of the day. The school usually had about fifty students in attendance. Tuition was $10.00 to $12.00 per year and was often paid in kind, but intelligent boys who were indigent were admitted free of charge. Some students at Caldwell's school were from as far away as Virginia or South Carolina. Five of them went on to become governors of their states; one of those governors was John Motley Morehead, governor of North Carolina from 1841 to 1845.

Most of the Presbyterian ministers in the western part of the Carolinas and Virginia studied under Caldwell. In 1795 he was offered the presidency of the University of North Carolina but declined to accept the offer. Earlier, having read extensively in medical books, Caldwell had become one of Guilford County's first physicians. He continued to heal, teach, and preach until he retired in 1820. David Caldwell died in 1824, an eyewitness to the first fifty years of Guilford County's history and its first prominent citizen.

At the outbreak of the American Revolution in 1775, the notion that any major military engagement could take place within the bounds of Guilford County probably never occurred to anyone. But for a brief moment in 1781 the conflict centered on the woods and fields around Guilford's ramshackle courthouse on the Salisbury road. The British army was brought to the "fatal field" at Guilford Courthouse as a result of a change in British strategy that occurred in 1778. The new British plan, which followed a three-year military standoff in the North, aimed at smothering the rebellion in America by conquering the South. By 1780 Georgia and South Carolina were in British hands. The British commander—Charles, Lord Cornwallis—was anxious to push into North Carolina and Virginia to regain those colonies for the crown. But his strategy received a severe setback in October 1780 at Kings Mountain when his left wing was crushed by American militia. Cornwallis then moved his army to Charlotte—at about the same time that General Nathanael Greene arrived to take over the Americans' southern command.

Nathanael Greene, one of Gen. George Washington's best field commanders and a logistician of extraordinary ability, devised a plan that led General Cornwallis into battle at Guilford Courthouse and ultimately to his defeat at Yorktown. Photograph of engraving from the Albert Barden Photograph Collection in custody of the Division of Archives and History.

Greene divided his force into two segments. To counter that ploy, Cornwallis divided his troops into three columns, the westernmost of which was mauled at Cowpens in South Carolina in January 1781. Despite that setback, Cornwallis was eager for a showdown battle and pursued Greene's smaller force into North Carolina. The Americans retreated northward, drawing the British further from their supply sources. Days of maneuvering in bitterly cold and wet weather followed, during which the two armies were seldom more than twenty miles apart. By mid-March Greene, having received requested reinforcements, had more than 4,000 militiamen and took up a favorable position on the ground at Guilford Courthouse. That body of troops constituted one of the largest colonial armies ever assembled in the South. Cornwallis, who continued to hunger for action, had by that time arrived at nearby Deep River Friends Meeting with some 2,200 men. The opportunity to destroy Greene's large force lured Cornwallis into a trap. On the afternoon of March 15 the two armies met in the Battle of Guilford Courthouse, a key military engagement that marked the beginning of the end of the Revolutionary War.

Why did Nathanael Greene select Guilford Courthouse as the site of the decisive battle? The answer lay in Greene's methods of operation. Greene hoped to avoid facing British regulars in the type of parade-ground battle so typical of the eighteenth century. Instead, he adopted the semi-guerrilla tactics of fight, retreat, and rise and fight again. To make those tactics succeed, Greene required three things of a battlefield: first, a known location that could easily be found by militiamen; second, a place in which the British would have to move through woods and into a final assault up a hill across a clearing; and third, a place in which the patriots would not be trapped by water as they departed. As his army had crossed the Carolinas in the winter of 1780-1781, Greene reconnoitered for such a place to do battle

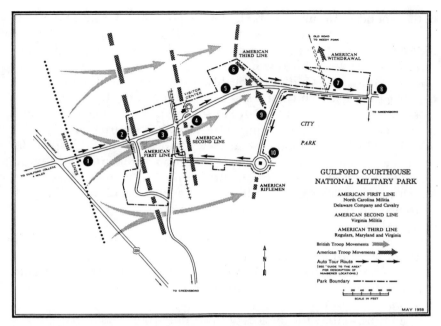

This map enables visitors to Guilford Courthouse National Military Park to conceptualize the bitter struggle that took place on the battlefield on the afternoon of March 15, 1781. The map depicts the three American battle lines. Map from *Guilford Courthouse National Military Park Handbook No. 30* (Washington: U.S. Government Printing Office, 1959).

with Cornwallis. He passed by Guilford Courthouse at least twice and studied the ground carefully. It had everything he needed.

Thus, it was toward Guilford Courthouse that Cornwallis's soldiers marched from Deep River Friends Meeting on the morning of March 15, 1781. The battle began just after one o'clock in the afternoon when the British and Greene's first line—which straddled the Salisbury road—exchanged volleys. The militiamen waiting in the woods were under orders to get off three rounds before retreating. A second line of militiamen deeper in the woods was reinforced with cannon and cavalry. A third line, manned by two brigades of Continentals, was on a rise above the clearing.

As the British assaulted those lines, deadly fire from the Americans cut them down. In a final effort to save the day at the third line, Cornwallis ordered his artillery to fire on his own men as they became mingled with the American regulars in hand-to-hand combat. After two hours of fighting, the British drove the rebels from the field and claimed victory.

It was no victory. Instead of a conquering force, all that remained of Cornwallis's army was a decimated, neutralized body of men. One-fourth of the British lay dead or wounded, while the patriots, of whom about 300 were lost, were preparing to "rise and fight again" at a nearby rallying point. The carnage around the courthouse was appalling, and the suffering

5

of the wounded was made worse by forty-eight hours of continuous rainfall. Greene's tactics had succeeded; Cornwallis had no choice but to retreat to Wilmington. There he planned the campaign that led to Virginia and eventual surrender at Yorktown.

Most residents of Guilford probably realized the importance of what happened in their county, and some had joined in the fray inasmuch as most adult males were required by law to serve in the militia. Participants included Quakers who, according to legend, went "squirrel hunting" that day. The Quaker meetinghouse at New Garden became a hospital for wounded from both sides, and some of the dead were buried in its graveyard. One can read the inscription "British and American Soldiers Buried March 1781 . . . Peace Good Will" on a stone there. Following the battle there was an outbreak of smallpox, but people soon returned to their normal lives.

In time nature restored the damage the battles had caused around the courthouse. Corn grew again in the fields, bullet nicks in trees healed, abandoned muskets rusted away, and cartridge boxes moldered in the mud. People still came to the place not to see the battlefield but because they had to. It was the county seat.

From time to time the justices of the county court had the courthouse repaired, and in 1785 they named the place Martinville to honor Alexander Martin, the first governor of North Carolina from Guilford. By that time Guilford was its present size. It was first partitioned in 1779 when Randolph County was created, and then again in 1785 to form Rockingham County. But no monuments were erected to the memory of the men who fought and died near the courthouse.

Martinville was abandoned after 1808 when the county seat was moved to Greensboro—then spelled Greensborough. The old courthouse and other buildings fell into decay, and the place was forgotten. What had happened at Guilford Courthouse in 1781 was one of the most significant events ever to occur in Guilford County, but many years passed before the battlefield came to be seen as a place that should be preserved and the events of March 15, 1781, remembered.

The most lasting local political development in the early national period was the decision to move the county seat away from Martinville. That decision came as a result of local political infighting in which a "centre party" favored the move, while others wanted to keep things as they were. The disagreement appears to have been between believers in some early form of progress and those who either had vested interests in Martinville or saw the move as an unnecessary expenditure. The county justices, who probably were tiring of problems connected with maintaining the 1774 courthouse, favored the "centre" faction, which took its name from a desire to move the county seat to the geographic center of the county—a point six miles southeast of Martinville that was said to be more accessible because of its location.

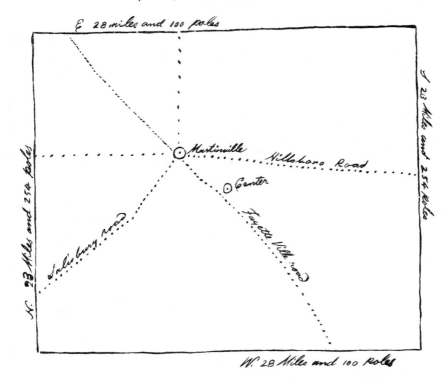

A committee appointed in 1807 to relocate the seat of Guilford County drew this crude map, which shows the county's geographic center; the following year that location was named in honor of Nathanael Greene. Map from McDaniel Lewis and James G. W. MacLamroc [comps.], *Basic Documents Relating to the Founding of Greensboro, North Carolina, Compiled for Its Sesquicentennial Celebration, May 2-10, 1958.*

The determination of the "centre party" to make the move prevailed. In 1808 the county justices appointed six commissioners to locate a new seat of government in the exact center of the county. A resulting survey showed that point to be in a swamp, so the justices located the county seat half a mile south—at the present intersection of Elm and Market streets in Greensboro. There they purchased forty-two acres for $92.00. By May 1809 a new courthouse was ready for use.

When it came to naming the new town, the commissioners honored Nathanael Greene—but the spelling went awry. The final *e* in Greene's name was lost in the legislative shuffle, and the name that emerged was Greensborough. The commissioners exhibited some imagination in naming the town, but the design they employed in laying it out on a plat was notably lacking in that quality. The design did not include a single square inch of public space other than the land to be used for streets. The court-house was placed squarely in the middle of the central intersection, almost as an afterthought. The lots were priced in relation to their respective distance from the courthouse, and all were sold. Thus, with virtually an unlimited amount of land at their disposal, the commissioners failed to think in terms of the future. Downtown Greensboro is still locked into their tightly drawn grid of narrow streets and an absence of public space.

N

| 16 Moses Lovet (Lovett) $5.01 | 15 Leven Kirkman $6.50 | 12 Leven Kirkman $6.50 | 11 Jesse Cook $8.25 | 9 Jesse Cook $10.05 | 10 Gray Booth $7.85 | 12 Nathan Mendenhall $7.63 |
| 14 Jonathan Ozment $4.80 | 13 Levi Huston (Houston) $5.50 | 10 Levi Tucker $10.02 | 9 Isaac Weatherly $22.80 | 7 Robert Ryan $40.77 | 8 Nathan Lester $ | 11 Nathan Mendenhall $5.50 |

[WEST GASTON STREET]   [EAST GASTON STREET]

| 8 John Macy $5.50 | 7 Dr. David Caldwell $5 | [NORTH GREENE STREET] | 4 Dr. David Caldwell $20 | 3 Isaiah Weatherly $50 | [NORTH ELM STREET] | 3 John Dillon $57 | 4 Levi Huston (Houston) $29.60 | [NORTH DAVIE STREET] | 6 Leven Kirkman $13.04 |
| 6 Nathan Mendenhall $20 | 5 Isaac Armfield $23 | | 2 Daniel Sullivan $57.25 | 1 William Ryan $151 | | 1 Levi Tucker $150 | 2 John M'Adow (McAdoo) $131 | | 5 Robert Donnell $47.50 |

W   E

[WEST MARKET STREET]   COURT HOUSE   [EAST MARKET STREET]

| 6 Thomas Caldwell $26 | 5 John Hoskins $52 | [SOUTH GREENE STREET] | 2 Samuel Sullivan $76 | 1 Thomas Bevell $139 | [SOUTH ELM STREET] | 1 Colonel Daniel Gillaspie (Gillespie) $136 | 2 Samuel Sullivan $102 | [SOUTH DAVIE STREET] | 5 Joseph Lovet (Lovett) $44 |
| 8 | 7 Richard Curtis $18.50 | | 4 | 3 Levi Huston (Houston) $52.50 | | 3 Robert Lindsay $52.50 | 4 David Maben (Mebane) $16.35 | | 6 Vincent Russom $10.26½ |

[WEST SYCAMORE STREET]   [EAST SYCAMORE STREET]

| 10 John Howell $18.50 | 9 James Parsons $22.50 | 7 Richard Lain (Lane) $15.01 | 8 William Armfield $7.25 |

NORTH

post oak

S

Having acquired 640 acres of land from Ralph Gorrell, the committee to relocate the county seat carved the tract into plats and offered them for sale as a means of raising money to finance a log courthouse, which the committee sited at the intersection of Elm and Market streets. Plat map from Lewis and MacLamroc, *Basic Documents Relating to the Founding of Greensboro.*

Even though the place was new, the practices and procedures of county government remained the same and were basically unchanged from colonial times. The court of pleas and quarter sessions was still the locus of power, although the General Assembly—and not the governor and his council, as in colonial days—appointed the justices. Some county offices, such as sheriff, were elective, but a small group of men held most of the power in the county. If men had fought and died at Guilford Courthouse for truly representative government, they did not find much of it after independence.

The form of county government remained largely unaltered until 1868, when a new state constitution went into effect. The justices continued to see to maintenance of roads, upkeep of the courthouse, supervision of records, and levying of taxes, which were collected by the sheriff. Records from the early period are sketchy, but it is known that Andrew Jackson, who was studying law in Guilford, was appointed a constable in 1789.

At that early time there was one matter of national importance that required the attention of the people. A convention met at Hillsborough in July 1788 to consider ratification of the new United States Constitution. Five delegates represented Guilford, including David Caldwell, and all voted to reject the document because it failed to include a bill of rights. In so doing, they voted with the majority at the convention. Subsequently, in November 1789, a different Guilford delegation voted with the majority to ratify the Constitution, with the understanding that a bill of rights would be added to the document.

Greensboro has been described as a "chosen center," placed in the middle of the county for political reasons, but the Quaker founders of Jamestown established that community for economic reasons. They were interested in harnessing the waters of the Deep River to saw wood, grind grain, and turn lathes as they created the county's first manufacturing facilities, small though they were. Nearby was William Beard's hat shop, where the wide-brimmed hats worn by many Quakers were made. By the late eighteenth century several brick buildings faced the federal road that ran through Jamestown, making it the first place in Guilford to have the appearance of a town. Jamestown was designated a polling place in the late 1790s and granted a state charter in 1812.

The early patterns of settlement in Guilford saw the best land quickly claimed, making it appear that the county was filled up. If one wanted good land and was not in line to inherit it, the best chances lay in the western United States, which had reached the Mississippi River in 1783. The growth of Guilford's population up to 1830 was steady but slow. In 1800 the county, by then its present size, had 9,442 people, a number that increased to 11,420 in 1810. By 1830 the population was 18,737, but even that modest gain was significant in North Carolina, a state that was barely holding its own in population. The nonwhite portion of the county's population amounted to about 13 percent, and Guilford had the second-largest number of white people in the state. People living in Guilford County during those decades found life stable and unchanging.

Virtually everyone was engaged in farming, but some did other work on the side. Hat maker William Beard would have been an extreme exception if all he did was make hats. Guilford's people produced a variety of things they needed for everyday use, and in enough quantity, for the census takers to note. The census of 1810 reported, for example, that 148,400 yards of cloth had been woven and 69,000 gallons of whiskey distilled during a one-year period. Inasmuch as 1,600 gallons of flaxseed oil were pressed during that period, one can conclude that most of the cloth was linen or linsey-woolsey. Other noteworthy products included hides and a small quantity of gunpowder. Interestingly, neither cotton nor tobacco figured in Guilford's early nineteenth-century economy.

In the early nineteenth century North Carolina was called the "Rip Van Winkle State." Guilford County in that era probably reflected some aspects of that characterization. But much had happened in the first seventy-five years. The land had gone from wilderness to active farms and developing towns. The apparatus of government was in place and assured orderly, if not fully representative, governance. There was a new, and growing, county seat. Religious groups enjoyed full freedom to express their beliefs. The county had given the state David Caldwell and the nation Dolley Madison, Guilford-born wife of James Madison, fourth president of the United States. But, living in what was then a "western" county, the people of Guilford could expect little succor from a North Carolina General Assembly dominated by conservative easterners who resisted the economic, educational, and constitutional reform desired by westerners. The only way to break that pattern would be for people of vision and force to place their fortunes and reputations on the line to bring about the developments they believed would awaken the state.

II
1830-1870

The period leading up to the Civil War was a time of continuing change in Guilford County. One of the most visible aspects of that change was the appearance in 1826 of the *Greensborough Patriot*, a weekly newspaper. The journal was the brainchild of William Swaim, a self-taught journalist who had grown up in the Centre community in southeastern Guilford. When Swaim established the paper, political conditions in North Carolina provided ample subject matter, and the young editor made it his business to point out relentlessly what ought to be done to modernize the state.

Swaim's list included some matters that concern even contemporary residents of Guilford County. Improvements in education were near the top of that list, and Swaim found plenty of room for change in everything from agricultural practices to banks, which then lacked knowledgeable officers interested in economic development. But no matter how much was done to create schools, raise better crops, or erect factories, Swaim knew that the key to the future lay in solving the long-standing problem of isolation. Swaim was advocating improved transportation facilities before railroads existed; he died in 1835 just as the first railroads were being built. His editorial efforts helped awaken people to the need to solve the state's transportation problems and led to the construction of the North Carolina Railroad in the 1850s.

Swaim lived to see an attempt at industrial development. In 1833 the *Patriot*, relying upon information published in the Pittsburgh *Pennsylvania Advocate*, reported that Henry Humphreys had purchased "a steam engine, for a cotton manufactory to be erected in the town of Greensborough, N.C." Word came that a "splendid building" would be erected to house the cotton factory and that Humphreys intended to produce 1,500 pounds of spun cotton each week. A year later the *Patriot* noted that the mill was in operation and that production would be increased to 3,000 pounds of yarn a week.

Humphreys issued scrip on which was pictured a four-story building, but it is questionable whether such a structure was ever built. The 1840 census lists a "cotton manufactory" in Greensboro with 2,500 spindles that

This scrip in the amount of "ONE DOLLAR," issued by Greensboro entrepreneur Henry Humphreys in 1837, bears the image of an early factory four stories tall. It is doubtful that a structure of such size existed in Greensboro at that time, but it illustrates Humphreys's dream of prosperity through industry. Photograph courtesy Greensboro Historical Museum, Greensboro.

produced goods valued at $50,000, but there is no description of the "manufactory" itself. It reportedly was located on the northern edge of Greensboro. Unfortunately, the Mount Hecla Mill, as the factory was known, was not destined to remain in the village. Problems in obtaining fuel proved insurmountable and forced Humphreys to abandon the project and to move the machinery to a waterpower site on the Yadkin River in the 1840s. Henry Humphreys, who paid for labor with worthless scrip, appears either to have been a man of prodigious but misguided vision or one of questionable character.

In the 1830s economic activity in Greensboro involved providing for thirsty and hungry clients of the county courthouse. A few people fashioned spokes and handles out of wood, but there was no group of potential factory hands. The industrialization of Guilford would require more than hopes and inspiration.

In the opening decades of the nineteenth century the absence of public schools forced parents to band together to provide means of educating their children. Under that system, parents pooled money to construct schools and pay teachers. These "old field schools" appeared in many places, but there was no supervision of the teaching that went on within their walls— nor were there any standards for teachers, facilities, or the length of the school term. The leading authority on Guilford County's schools estimates that by the 1840s at least forty such schools existed. The average cost per child was $2.00 a quarter, and the curriculum consisted of the three R's. The only incentive to send a child to those schools was the parents' interest in education, and only about a quarter of the school-age population attended. One-third of the people were literate. To some of North Carolina's political leaders, it was a pathetic and intolerable situation.

By the late 1830s change was in the air. In 1839 the North Carolina General Assembly enacted a law that permitted people to vote on the question of whether or not they wanted to have tax-supported public schools. Guilford was among the first counties to take advantage of that provision and voted by a margin of 1,550 to 422 to establish such schools. In 1841 a county court-appointed school board created school districts in the county, and the first public school opened in Greensboro in July 1841. Toward the end of the 1840s about 40 percent of all school-age children attended those institutions. The schools received financial support from a tax of 5 cents per $100 worth of real property, along with a "head tax" of ten cents on each adult white male. The so-called "common" schools did not solve the problem of illiteracy, but they placed Guilford County in the forefront of educational developments of the time.

Two of Guilford's citizens—Nereus Mendenhall and Calvin H. Wiley—made signal contributions to education in North Carolina. Mendenhall believed that it was important to examine the "mental and moral qualifications" of prospective teachers and became Guilford's first teacher examiner. Subsequently he convinced the North Carolina General Assembly to require the certification of teachers throughout the state. Wiley became North Carolina's first superintendent of public instruction. Although lack of

Calvin Henderson Wiley (1819-1887), North Carolina's first superintendent of public instruction, worked to improve the quality of teaching and to lengthen the school term in the state's public schools. Photograph of engraving from the Albert Barden Photograph Collection.

funds forced him to work out of his home and pay for his own travel, he improved teacher quality and lengthened the state's school term. The Civil War badly damaged Guilford's schools. After the war Wiley was proscribed from holding public office because he had held such an office with the state government under the Confederacy.

One type of educational institution that augmented the common schools was the private academy, which usually was operated by a religious denomination. These were schools for teenagers, at which girls received a "finishing" and the boys were prepared for enrollment at the University of North Carolina. There were at least twenty-six academies in Guilford County prior to the Civil War, and three have survived to the present. One such institution is Greensboro College, a Methodist school for girls that opened in 1846 and prospered until fire destroyed its main building in 1863. After the fire, Greensboro College moved to several locations before returning to its original site, where it remains. The other two survivors are New Garden Boarding School, opened in 1837 by the Society of Friends (Quakers), and Oak Ridge Institute, opened in 1853. New Garden Boarding School never closed during the Civil War and in 1887 became Guilford College—the first degree-granting institution in the county. Money donated by British and northern Quakers facilitated the survival of New Garden Boarding School. Oak Ridge Institute went out of existence during the Civil War but was revived in 1875 as Oak Ridge Military Academy.

Growth of Guilford's population base was limited to the natural increase of births over deaths until well into the nineteenth century. By 1860 the population of 20,056 was slightly more than double that of 1800, when the total was 9,442—a trend in line with that of the state as a whole.

The people who lived in Guilford County in the mid-nineteenth century soon experienced changes beyond anything they might have imagined. In the mid-1850s the locomotive whistles of the North Carolina Railroad (NCRR) interrupted the slumber of "Ancient Guilford," as some called the county. One of the leaders in the movement that brought about that development was John Motley Morehead, Greensboro's leading citizen, who served as governor of North Carolina from 1841 to 1845. He went from rural Guilford to Greensboro as a young lawyer in the 1820s and soon augmented his law practice with dry goods and grocery businesses. Interested in anything new, he also imported and sold labor-saving mechanical devices. Morehead was committed to ending central North Carolina's isolation and believed that railroads were the answer. He became the first president of the NCRR and solved many of its early financial problems.

Construction of the NCRR began in Greensboro in July 1851 with the driving of a symbolic first spike and a speech by Calvin Graves of Caswell County, who, as president of the North Carolina Senate, cast the deciding vote by which the NCRR's charter was approved—by a vote of 23 to 22—on January 25, 1849. Track-laying then commenced at the projected line's

John Motley Morehead (1796-1866), instrumental in constructing the North Carolina Railroad, served as president of the road during its formative period. He subsequently served as governor of North Carolina, 1841-1845, and was the last resident of Guilford County to be elected to that office. Portrait of Morehead (ca. 1856) by William Garl Browne; reproduced in Laura MacMillan, comp., *The North Carolina Portrait Index, 1700-1860* (Chapel Hill: University of North Carolina Press, 1963), 166.

western terminus at Charlotte and eastern terminus at Goldsboro and proceeded toward Greensboro. On January 29, 1856, workmen placed the line's last rail. Few developments since that time have had as profound an effect on Guilford County, and the rejoicing that took place when the first train appeared was fully justifiable.

RAILROADS IN NORTH CAROLINA
1850

WILMINGTON AND RALEIGH RAILROAD
RALEIGH AND GASTON RAILROAD
NORTH CAROLINA RAILROAD (BEING PROJECTED)

The crescent-shaped broken line connecting Goldsboro and Charlotte by way of Hillsborough, Greensboro, and Salisbury is the route followed by the North Carolina Railroad. At Goldsboro the road linked North Carolina's landlocked interior to the existing north-south Wilmington and Weldon Railroad. Map from Cecil Kenneth Brown, *A State Movement in Railroad Development . . .* (Chapel Hill: University of North Carolina Press, 1928), 75.

One of the most remarkable, but perhaps not unexpected, results of the end of isolation came in agriculture. The census of 1850 reported a total output of 1,900 pounds of tobacco in Guilford County, while in 1860 that total was an astounding 724,348 pounds. While agriculture was

In this photograph can be seen the considerable railroad-related activity that took place in Greensboro in the 1890s. The building with the overhanging roof at right was Greensboro's first railroad station, built in 1856. It was demolished in the 1920s to make way for an underpass. Photograph courtesy Greensboro Historical Museum.

predominant, the census takers also listed as residents of Guilford a number of artisans who worked in wood or leather, as well as several gunsmiths. During the Civil War Guilford County's gunsmiths produced rifles and carbines for the Confederate army.

Another direct result of the advent of the railroad came at the place in Guilford County where a survey revealed that the tracks would intersect with the existing plank road that connected Fayetteville and Salem. That place was the highest point on the rail line, 912 feet above sea level. The potential offered by such a location led speculators to buy the land around the projected crossing. In December 1853 one speculator sold his landholdings at public auction, with lots fronting rail property going for the highest price.

Track-laying crews pushing north and east from Charlotte reached the plank road on November 22, 1855, bringing forth a large crowd of curious people to greet the train. By 1859 the crossing had become a town that boasted 525 people, 2 hotels, 2 churches, and 7 stores. Under the name "High Point," the town, two miles square, received a state charter in May 1859.

The increase in tobacco production and the emergence of High Point were the most obvious immediate results of the arrival of the NCRR. But of equally great importance was the fact that the future looked different. The

16

market economy, which was beginning to develop, no longer would be hampered by the problem of access to the outside world. Although the future seemed bright in 1860, there were war clouds on the horizon, and war would serve as the catalyst for the next changes.

Slaveholding was not a major activity in Guilford, and the county's Quaker population had long opposed the practice. Most of the county's people were small farmers whose interests were different from those prevalent in eastern North Carolina; Guilford's people had even less in common with the plantation economies of the lower South. One student of the county's history asserts that Guilford was controlled during the pre-Civil War period primarily by attorneys who also were part-time businessmen and farmers. John Motley Morehead is a perfect example of the type. These men began to acquire power in the 1840s. While cautious and conservative, and not always in agreement on political issues, these lawyer/businessmen were united on the idea of economic progress and were well positioned to benefit from such progress. The North Carolina Railroad was exactly in line with their desires—secession and war were not.

If antislavery Quakers and others could see no reason to secede, neither could the "strategic elite." They belonged to an emerging world of contracts and commerce that valued continuity, not conflict. Thus, secession was not popular in Guilford, and in early 1861 the citizens defeated by a margin of 2,771 to 113 a proposal to call a convention to consider secession. Two leading citizens—John Motley Morehead and Congressman John Adams Gilmer—sought peace. Morehead went to Washington as a peace commissioner, and Gilmer made a plea for union on the floor of the

Congressman John Adams Gilmer (1805-1868), a resident of Greensboro, worked without success to preserve the Union during the secession crisis of 1860-1861. Photograph of engraving from the files of the Division of Archives and History.

17

United States House of Representatives. At first the *Greensborough Patriot* reflected unionism and a desire for peace.

After Fort Sumter, and following Lincoln's call for 75,000 volunteers, there was a short-term burst of enthusiasm for secession and war. The *Patriot* reversed itself and urged secession by legislative act rather than through the convention, which took the state out of the Union in May. A volunteer company, the Guilford Grays, was raised and sent to Fort Macon. The justices of the county court appropriated $50,000 to equip additional volunteer units to "repel invasion." But it was not long before the same justices were begging Richmond for help in caring for families of men in the army. A severe drought in 1863 and 1864 created a food shortage, but nothing deterred Confederate requisitioning parties from seizing provisions. An additional and unexpected problem emerged when people were stranded after being forcibly removed from railroad trains commandeered by the military in Greensboro.

Enthusiasm for the war evaporated, and Guilford became a county in which peace meetings were held and William W. Holden, the Peace party candidate for governor of North Carolina in 1864, gained considerable support. It was common knowledge that deserters and draft resisters were hiding out in the area, and tensions rose as military units were dispatched to capture them.

The troubles and dislocation caused by war were nothing compared to the benefit that came to Guilford when the Confederate government built the Piedmont Railroad to connect Greensboro and Danville, Virginia. The rail line, built as a "matter of national defense," has been described as "the most significant improvement made in the entire Confederate railroad system." By filling in what was then a "missing link" in the track between Columbia, South Carolina, and Danville, the Confederates created a valuable supply line and in the process changed the entire pattern of rail traffic for the future.

To some, logic had long indicated that the missing link should be built. Morehead and others favored the line, while opposition came from those who feared that North Carolina's products would be funneled outside the state and into Virginia. When the war came, opponents of the line lost to the argument of military necessity. Even Governor Zebulon B. Vance, who opposed the link, had no choice but to support the Piedmont Railroad. Construction began in April 1863 and, in May 1864, when the first train headed north, there were some residents of Guilford who knew their cause had triumphed.

In April 1865 Jefferson Davis, escaping the threatened Confederate capital of Richmond, took the Piedmont Railroad to Greensboro, where he held a cabinet meeting in a boxcar near the Elm Street crossing. Because Union raiders had burned a railroad bridge at Jamestown, the Confederate president continued southward by wagon. The brief presence in Greensboro of Davis and his cabinet provided material for persistent stories to the effect that the retreating Confederates had buried quantities of gold there. Meanwhile, Guilford County was inundated by soldiers from General Joseph E. Johnston's retreating army. After the surrender a total of 38,718 of them was paroled in Greensboro.

About 1,500 men from Guilford served in the Confederate army, but the county was the site of only a few minor skirmishes. There was violence there in April 1865 when rioting broke out in Greensboro as a mob smashed into a quartermaster warehouse to seize food and blankets. Confederate troops easily quelled the disturbance. Some hard feelings existed toward merchants who had profited from the war, but recovery was fairly rapid. The NCRR was soon back in operation. Apparently there was little disruption to the economic and political power structure, except that younger lawyer/entrepreneurs began to replace their older counterparts, with whom the younger men shared generally the same beliefs and ambitions.

Guilford's citizens now had to deal with the results of the war. Some had to swallow the bitter pill of defeat, which was not an easy task. Others were relieved that the war was over and that the heavy hand of the Confederacy, with its constant requisitions and efforts to control words and deeds, was gone. But those who experienced the greatest change were the people who had been slaves. There were about 4,500 former slaves in Guilford who began new lives without assistance other than the aid they received from the Freedmen's Bureau. They moved about, adopted new names, and began to try to find their way in life. Scarcity of food was a major problem until the Freedmen's Bureau provided relief. Shelter was likewise a problem for those who departed or were forced off farms in Guilford. Many freedmen gravitated toward towns.

In Greensboro, Yardley Warner, an agent of the Association of Friends of Philadelphia for the Relief of Colored Freedmen, aided the former bondsmen. Warner acquired 35 acres of land on the southern fringes of the town, divided the land into tracts, and sold the parcels at prices varying from $25.00 to $400 each. The plan was for the residents to obtain ownership of a house with space for a garden. Warner established a school, and many freedmen found work in small woodworking shops or in the developing dried fruit business. Warner subsequently returned to Pennsylvania, while his experiment, an early example of a planned subdivision, grew in size and population and later was annexed to Greensboro. In the 1960s the site, still known as Warnersville, became the location of three public housing projects, two of them sponsored by churches.

In the immediate postwar period the presence of strangers black and white, among them paroled soldiers who remained in Guilford, led to a belief that danger was everywhere and that the freedmen were a menace. In July 1865 the Guilford County court issued a call for order and loyalty to the Union. The court created a countywide police force, using as precincts the county's eighteen "captains' districts," which had been created in the antebellum era to aid in the administration of militia musters and the collecting of taxes.

President Andrew Johnson's appointment of William W. Holden as provisional governor of North Carolina pleased those residents of Guilford County who had supported Holden's regular candidacy for governor in 1864. After a constitutional convention, held in October 1865, repealed the ordinance of secession, abolished slavery, repudiated the state's war debt, and provided for November elections, it appeared that life would return to normal. Such a return to normality was certainly the hope of the former Democrats—by then known as Conservatives—many of whom were worried about the activities of the Freedmen's Bureau. This state of affairs changed dramatically in 1867 when Congress placed North Carolina, along with the rest of the South, under the provisions of the First Reconstruction Act.

One resident of Guilford County became one of the most famous of all the so-called "carpetbaggers"—northern-born white Republicans who came south during and after the Civil War—Albion W. Tourgée. A Union army officer, lawyer, and author, Tourgée came to North Carolina from Ohio in the autumn of 1865 attracted by the salubrious climate and the hope of economic opportunity and gain. He went into business as a nurseryman west of Greensboro and employed a number of freedmen. Tourgée soon found that many of his neighbors were unionists of long standing and ripe for political organization. Realizing the possibilities for political gain, he became the driving force for the Union League, an organization that sought to promote the policies of the Radical Republicans, in Guilford, Alamance, and Orange counties.

Tourgée became determined to see justice afforded the freedmen, but most unionists did not share that view. Moreover, Tourgée was critical of his fellow unionists for submitting to secession and the Confederacy. At a loyalist convention in Philadelphia in the fall of 1866, Tourgée incurred the lasting enmity of many of Guilford's citizens, both unionist and Conservative, when he delivered a speech on the mistreatment of blacks in Guilford that included an unsubstantiated report that the bodies of fifteen blacks had been found in a pond. On returning home, he was threatened with death and came to be viewed as a fanatic.

The enmity increased in January 1867 when Tourgée began publishing a newspaper known as the *Union Register*, in which he called for the disfranchisement of anyone who had participated voluntarily in the rebellion. Tourgée repeatedly attacked moderate unionists who did not support his views. After six months the *Union Register* suspended publication. Tourgée became a delegate to the 1868 state constitutional convention, at which he was elected chief marshal and chairman of the Republican executive committee. Much of the phraseology of the Reconstruction constitution has been credited to Tourgée. While the document shocked Conservatives, it was a blueprint for modern, progressive, and democratic government.

North Carolina's 1868 constitution contributed signally to the reorganization of county government. Provisions in the document abolished the county courts and replaced them with elected five-member boards of commissioners. It also instituted in North Carolina the township plan of local government. The General Assembly divided every county into townships of approximately equal size to be governed by elected clerks, justices of the peace, and school committees. In Guilford, eighteen townships replaced the old captains' districts. The township plan was designed to broaden public participation in government. While townships had worked successfully as a means of governance in states such as Pennsylvania and Iowa, they were soon abandoned in North Carolina. Guilford County presently recognizes its eighteen townships, but they serve mainly to help locate parcels of real estate.

In March 1868 Albion Tourgée was elected a judge of the North Carolina Superior Court and served on a committee to revise the state's civil code. In Greensboro he worked to expand educational opportunities for black women and was active in the local bar association. He was a delegate to the state constitutional convention of 1875, only to see Conservatives return control of county government to the county courts, with the justices appointed by the legislature.

Tourgée left North Carolina in 1879 and published two novels about his experiences during Reconstruction: *A Fool's Errand, By One of the Fools* and *Bricks without Straw*, both set in Guilford County. They were the only novels about Reconstruction that were based on contemporaneous firsthand experiences. Tourgée's opinion of Guilford was that it was one of the "most prosperous, attractive, and promising localities in the South" and should "become the seat of vast and valuable manufactures." If Guilford had not welcomed Tourgée, it did embrace subsequent newcomers, including veterans of the Union army, who helped create the factories that sprang up in the county and made North Carolina the most industrialized state in the South by the end of the nineteenth century.

III
1870-1920

In 1872 a new three-story brick courthouse with columns and an imposing bell tower stood on the northwest corner of Elm and Market streets, having replaced Guilford County's fourth courthouse, which had been destroyed by fire earlier that year, resulting in the loss of most of the county's records. The 1872 structure remained the locus of county government until it was replaced in 1918. For the first time, open space could be found in downtown Greensboro around the courthouse, where people could relax and watch the passing scene—which, by the end of the nineteenth century, was beginning to reflect rapid change.

From 1870 to 1920 Guilford County went from agrarian/rural to industrial/urban as Greensboro and High Point took their places among the larger cities of the state. The growth and development of interior cities such as Greensboro and High Point has been seen as one of the most significant developments in the late nineteenth-century South. By the early years of the twentieth century Guilford was on a different course from most of its neighboring counties. In 1870 the population of the county was 21,736; by 1920 it was 79,272, with more than 75 percent of its people residing in the two cities.

Until 1895 county government did not reflect the changes that were taking place. In that year the North Carolina General Assembly returned to the people the right to elect county commissioners by direct vote. Such elections commenced in Guilford in 1898. By then, activity there centered on events in Greensboro and High Point. The cities and their leaders sought to be in the forefront of change and began to promote urban development and industrial growth. The political leadership of the two municipalities, with its generally progressive attitudes concerning racial peace and industrial development and its emphasis on progress, served to typify the two cities as "New South" communities.

By 1906 ambitious residents of High Point began questioning the wisdom of remaining in the same county with Greensboro, asserting that their city should be the seat of a new county. That attitude came from a feeling that High Point was outgrowing its subordinate place in Guilford and would soon be as big, if not bigger, than Greensboro. For some citizens of

The fifth Guilford County Courthouse stood from 1872 to 1918 at the northwest corner of Elm and Market streets, the present site of the Jefferson-Pilot building. The structure was demolished after a new courthouse was erected two blocks away. View of courthouse, made from a picture postcard, from the files of the Division of Archives and History.

High Point, justice required that the growing town be in a separate county. There was also a political argument to the effect that High Point was a Republican town that was being outvoted by Democratic Greensboro. In 1910 there emerged a movement to create a new county from the southern portion of Guilford. A bill to accomplish such a scheme reached the General Assembly in 1911 but was defeated. The subject has resurfaced from time to time, most recently in 1979.

Despite or because of the rivalry, Guilford's rapidly growing cities were the key to the county's future. The evolution of Greensboro in the 1870-1920 period has been presented as an example of the rise of a New South city with a well-diversified economy and rapid growth. In 1870 the General Assembly officially chartered Greensboro as a municipality. One of the keys to Greensboro's rise was that new faces kept appearing among its governing elite. Greensboro's prospering manufacturers and merchants welcomed newcomers into the power structure. As a result, a more diverse set of leaders, and not a static group of old-line residents, emerged to direct local affairs.

The new leadership group began by creating a chamber of commerce in 1877 and went on to develop a long list of new organizations such as an industrial and immigration association, a tobacco association, a merchants association, a women's club, a charitable association, and a social welfare league. Within such groups, newcomers mixed with old-timers to gain recognition and acceptance in positions of leadership. The newcomers in turn helped to alter popular perceptions of the proper role and scope of local government. Greensboro thus received an infusion of new blood as its leaders worked energetically to push bond issues and mobilize public support for the improvement and development of public services. Some of the milestones in that process included the establishment of a school board (1890), a board of health (1902), a fire commission (1906), a street commission (1907), and a water and light commission (1910). Significantly, Greensboro in 1911 abandoned the aldermanic system in favor of the commissioner system of city government in a move that made problem solving more manageable.

While in some other cities old elites withdrew from civic activity as immigrant groups moved in, Greensboro saw them absorb the new as they worked together. The city depended heavily upon that process as it went from a village of about 2,000 people to a city of 19,861 between 1870 and 1920. One outsider who rose to prominence as a lawyer and politician during those years was Aubrey Lee Brooks. In his autobiography, Brooks wrote: "The beginning of the twentieth century brought Greensboro new life and opened new vistas. It was a desirable place in which to live."

As a lawyer, Brooks was a member of an important component of the power structure and a group particularly involved in bringing about change. While the lawyers might disagree on politics, they were united on economic goals, the central feature of which was industrialization. Living in a world of "contract and commerce," Guilford's lawyers were attuned to changes taking place elsewhere—changes that helped make North Carolina the industrial leader of the South by 1900.

Woven into the work of those people was the booster spirit. Civic-minded leaders picked up favorable items about their cities and spread them across newspapers and rehashed them in pamphlets and other publications. In an 1891 speech, North Carolina Governor Thomas M. Holt added his contribution to boosterism by characterizing Greensboro as a "community enlightened and progressive beyond average." There was curiosity about what was happening in Guilford, and in 1900 the *Wilmington Star* sent a reporter to find out what was going on. The reporter commented that the last time he had seen Greensboro it had no mills, but "now there is nothing but hustling and progress." Out of such material local boosters developed the theme that Guilford was the "best county" and its county seat the "best city" in the state. The idea could be carried to extremes, as when the *Greensboro Record* boasted on its masthead that Guilford was "The Land of Perpetual Spring"; several exceptionally hard freezes brought that claim into question, however.

Such boosterism was typical of the times in many places, and Greensboro's claim that the town's spirit was "getting things done as quickly as possible" could be said of dozens of other towns. Yet, when combined with the claim that Greensboro's "growth was always sane and solid," and when viewed in light of the industrialization that was beginning to take place, there was solid evidence that change was in the air.

The first stirrings toward industrialization came in High Point. A community of approximately 550 people in 1870, High Point grew rapidly with the rise of furniture manufacturing in the 1880s. The industry drew on nearby hardwood forests for raw materials. The earliest factories were small structures, usually operated under the supervision of experienced northerners and manned by people who left farms and were eager to find steady

This tranquil early twentieth-century view of Main Street in High Point belies the dynamism of the city's furniture industry, which had developed there in the 1880s and subsequently made the High Point area the nation's foremost center for the manufacture and marketing of furniture. Photograph from Holt McPherson, *High Pointers of High Point* (High Point: Hall Printing Company, 1976), 45.

employment. It required relatively little capital to turn out the plain bureaus, beds, and chairs that were in great demand in the nation's growing cities. By the turn of the century, furniture was being shipped out of High Point in trainloads.

Local entrepreneurs soon began to realize that the quality of their furniture equaled or exceeded that made in the North. In order to compete in a wider market and to take a position of leadership in the industry, the manufacturers established an organized display system. The results can be seen today in the International Home Furnishings Center (IHFC) in High Point, which originated as the Southern Furniture Exposition Building.

The idea for such a building came from J. J. Farris, editor of the *High Point Enterprise*, who suggested it in 1911. Exhibitions were already being held in the Broad Street Furniture Exposition Building, the Millis Building on South Main Street, and in the upstairs rooms of some factories. The need to institutionalize the exhibition process was obvious to the newly formed Southern Furniture Manufacturers' Association, headquartered in High Point. The association's first executive director, James T. Ryan, led the movement to create a central display building that would enable High Point to develop as the southern regional market.

High Point's manufacturers pooled their resources and in June 1919 acquired for $35,000 a lot on South Main Street, on which they began construction of a ten-story, $1 million structure with 261,000 square feet of exhibit space. The building opened in June 1921, by which time High Point's population was nearly 15,000. That year more than 700 furniture buyers visited the Exposition Building, where 149 exhibits were on display. The opening of the building coincided with the beginning of an era of prosperity in the 1920s as ever increasing numbers of furniture buyers came to High Point. Efforts by other cities to "capture" the furniture market have always failed, and the IHFC is presently the largest structure of its type in the world.

The industrialization of Guilford moved into high gear in 1895 when Moses and Ceasar Cone, owners of the Cone Export and Commission Company, a cotton goods marketing organization, began constructing their Proximity Mill, the first of the Cone mills, near Greensboro. Four years earlier the Cones had decided to enter the textile business in the South, where for more than a decade they had been wholesale grocery and tobacco distributors. In their transactions they often had been paid in bolts of cloth from small local mills. Finding that the cloth sold readily, they saw the potential for production and bought an interest in cotton mills in Asheville, Salisbury, and Gibsonville. One of their hopes was to manufacture a

In the years between 1890 and 1910 the forerunner of Cone Mills Corporation erected north of Greensboro the largest denim and flannel mills in the world, assuring Greensboro's future as an industrial center. Photograph from stereopticon view supplied by Cone Mills Corporation, Greensboro.

product of better quality than the loosely woven fabric they had been receiving in trade. The brothers saw an industry that was glutted and suffering from cutthroat competition. Perceiving the need for a strong marketing organization, they chartered the Cone Export and Commission Company, which initially was headquartered in New York but later moved to Greensboro because of the city's excellent transportation facilities and "proximity" to the South's cotton fields.

By the mid-1890s the Cone brothers had convinced 90 percent of the South's mill owners of the need for their services. Organizing a large financial and marketing operation had not been simple, but the Cone Export and Commission Company was soon earning about five cents on each dollar of gross receipts. It saved a number of mills from going under in the hard times of the 1890s and helped many manufacturers improve the quality of their cloth.

In 1896 the first denim rolled off the looms of the Proximity Mill, and four years later the Cones joined with Emanuel and Herman Sternberger to construct the first cotton flannel mill in the South. That facility, named the Revolution Cotton Mill, utilized newly invented processes and led to the boast: "World Leadership in Flannel." In 1905 the giant White Oak plant near Greensboro began production. It remains the world's largest denim mill. Moses Cone died in 1908, but the company continued to expand. In 1912 it opened the Proximity Print Works, the first textile printing plant of its type in the South.

An important feature of the Cone operations until the late 1940s was the mill village. The Cones constructed four such villages, which a New York reporter described as "Spotless Towns." The villages included a total of 1,600 houses, of which 400 were reserved for black workers. In 1915 families rented three-, four-, or six-room houses by the month for a dollar a room; the rent included electricity and water. In those tightly knit communities practically every need of a family was met. A dairy farm and abattoir provided the milk and meat sold in company stores. The company sold wood and coal to employees at below cost. Churches, built with Cone financial support, were complemented by a YMCA at which membership dues were seventy-five cents a year. The company also helped maintain public schools and provided a "welfare department." The latter was a combination home economics and health agency that in 1910 employed six welfare workers and three trained nurses. In 1923 all the Cone mill villages became part of Greensboro when the city expanded its limits. After World War II the mill village was no longer feasible or desirable, and by 1959 the last remaining dwellings were sold to employees of the mills.

The rise of insurance companies, wholesalers, and light industry and the constant expansion of retail business paralleled the growth of industrialization in Greensboro and in High Point. In 1895 there were no insurance

As what one writer for a northern newspaper characterized as "spotless towns," Cone mill villages included such amenities as picnics, nursing care, social workers, a YMCA, and company-supported schools and churches. These Cone workers are enjoying a company Fourth of July picnic. Photograph (ca. 1915) courtesy Cone Mills Corporation.

companies with home offices in Greensboro; by 1911 there were five, with combined total assets of $4.5 million. That rapid growth led to the claim that Greensboro was the "Hartford of the South" and that it led Atlanta and all other southern cities in the successful conduct of home insurance enterprises. A culminating moment came in 1912 when Security Life of Greensboro and Jefferson Standard Life of Raleigh merged and made Greensboro the home office. By 1916 Jefferson Standard, under the leader-

As president of Jefferson Standard Life Insurance Company, Julian Price was instrumental in Greensboro's development as the headquarters city for numerous life and casualty insurance companies. Photograph courtesy Jefferson-Pilot Life Insurance Company, Greensboro.

ship of Julian Price, had $46 million worth of insurance in force and was planning to erect a high-rise building. Insurance company headquarters helped to change the dress of people on the streets and demonstrated that Greensboro was no longer a country town. Best of all, it was said that the insurance enterprises were "a product of Southern Brains and Southern Money."

Wholesale houses first appeared in Greensboro in the 1870s, primarily because of the city's rail connections. The earliest of those establishments specialized in groceries, hardware, and dry goods. By the turn of the century eighteen wholesale businesses were in Greensboro, making it an important center for distribution and jobbing in the northern Piedmont.

One light industry that developed in Greensboro in the early twentieth century was cigar manufacturing. In 1911, for instance, fifteen million cigars were manufactured from Philippine tobacco as Greensboro became second only to Tampa in cigar production in the South. The cigar industry declined in the mid-twentieth century when modern production machinery could not be fitted into the old cigar company buildings in downtown Greensboro.

One of the desires of Guilford's leaders and boosters in the late nineteenth century was to become the hub of a network of railroads. With railroad tracks branching out in six directions by 1890, Greensboro appeared to be on the verge of becoming such a hub, but in the long run only the east-west and north-south rail lines proved strong. It was hoped that a rail line could be built over the Appalachian Mountains to the Middle West. Although the Yadkin and Atlantic line reached Mount Airy, it never crossed the mountains. Nevertheless, the high hopes of the 1870-1920 period brought the claim that Greensboro was "the railroad gateway to North Carolina," which was shortened to the term "Gate City," words still used today.

Good rail connections meant that products of the textile mills and furniture factories of Guilford moved easily and quickly to their destinations. Carloadings remained high, even during slack times nationally, and some of the finest passenger trains in the nation traversed Guilford. During World War I the United States Railway Administration completed the Pomona Yard near Greensboro. The yard included a roundhouse and shops, which enhanced Greensboro's position on the Southern Railway's main line between Washington and Atlanta. Construction of the Pomona Yard represented the second time that Guilford's railways had benefited from a war.

One of the most successful short rail lines in the state was the High Point, Thomasville, and Denton Railroad, the origins of which lay in the desire among early twentieth century High Point businessmen and civic leaders to create a direct competitor to the Southern Railway. The High Point, Thomasville, and Denton began in 1903 as a line for hauling rock from a

The Southern Railway station of 1898—presently the division headquarters for the Norfolk Southern line—was the scene of visits to Greensboro by Theodore Roosevelt, Woodrow Wilson, and W. E. B. Du Bois. Du Bois noted that the building's public facilities were an "exception" to what he generally encountered in the Jim Crow South. Photograph from James W. Albright, *Greensboro, 1808-1904: Facts, Figures, Traditions and Reminiscences* (Greensboro: Joseph J. Stone and Company, 1904), 71.

quarry at Glen Anna, near Thomasville. In 1907 a group of New York investors purchased the line's right-of-way, reorganized it as the Carolina Valley Railroad, and extended the tracks southward to Denton. The New Yorkers regraded the roadbed and installed heavier rails. Their long-term ambitions included electrified interurban passenger service northward to Greensboro, westward to Winston, and southeastward to Rockingham and Wadesboro and construction of a dam on the Yadkin River to generate the electricity required for such an enterprise. A financial recession that began in 1907 dashed these hopes, however.

In 1909 W. N. Coler and Company of New York acquired the Carolina Valley road and in June 1914 inaugurated passenger and freight service; the first item of freight was a desk manufactured by High Point's Myrtle Desk Company and shipped to Palatka, Florida. A monthly interest charge of $5,000, combined with complications growing out of World War I, forced the rail line into receivership until the 1920s. At that time another group of High Point businessmen, led by O. Arthur Kirkman, Sr., "took an old railroad with not much more than a streak of rust for rails" and made it into one of the most successful short lines in the state. The High Point, Thomasville, and Denton Railroad, as the line became known in 1924, remained independent until 1960, when the Southern Railway and the Seaboard Air Line Railway acquired it, divided its assets, and began operating it jointly.

If rail transportation was improved in the late nineteenth and early twentieth centuries, public roads were a different matter, inasmuch as township road overseers were still obliged to conscript able-bodied men to remove obstacles from and maintain public roads. Numerous descriptions of road conditions during inclement weather tell of near total immobilization in a sea of mud. Such conditions gave impetus to the so-called "Good Roads Movement," in which Guilford was in the forefront. By 1910 an "all-weather" gravel roadway connected High Point and Greensboro. But the key to better roads lay in ending the policy of attempting to maintain them with citizen labor. Not until the early 1920s, when the state began to assume responsibility for maintaining the state's public roads, did Guilford begin to be lifted out of the mire.

The booster spirit can be easily ridiculed, but it helps to heighten morale and creates a stronger sense of civic duty. It is a building block of municipal life that brings on change, creates jobs, and develops stronger services. No reasonable person would believe all the claims that are made, but the boosters' hyperbole contains elements of truth and points in the direction of the way things should be.

Perhaps the best examples of the effects of boosterism came in the early 1890s when the state announced plans to establish two new colleges—one for women and one for blacks. The locations of the proposed institutions were "up for grabs" in a competition that would award the schools to the highest bidder. To be chosen as the site for either college would require an unprecedented effort on the part of a local civic group. In a decision that proved to be one of the most significant developments in the history of Guilford County, the state ultimately awarded both institutions to Greensboro.

In 1891 the state selected Greensboro as the location for the Agricultural and Mechanical College for the Negro Race, forerunner of North Carolina A&T State University, and required from the city a donation in the amount of $8,000 in cash and a suitable location. Greensboro's leaders quickly moved to meet both requirements, and by 1893 the college's staff and students had arrived in Greensboro. Newspapers reported that the new institution would infuse approximately $25,000 a year into the local economy. Under the leadership of James B. Dudley, who became president of the institution in 1896, the college sought to provide practical education to its students, who would then "be able to raise the standard of living among their people."

Also in 1891 the state established and awarded to Greensboro the Normal and Industrial School for Women, forerunner of the University of North Carolina at Greensboro. The state had required communities interested in becoming the home of that institution to raise $30,000 through a bond issue and to donate a suitable location. When the result of the successful vote on the bond issue was announced, there was rejoicing in the streets of Greensboro and repeated blasts from locomotive and factory whistles. The school opened in October 1892 under the leadership of Charles D. McIver (known as "the steam engine in breeches") and offered programs in business, domestic science, and teacher training. In 1896 the word "college" was substituted for "school," and the institution awarded its first degrees in 1906.

Foust Hall at the North Carolina Normal and Industrial School for Women was completed in 1892. As the institution matured under the leadership of Charles D. McIver, its name was changed to North Carolina College for Women. The school is now known as the University of North Carolina at Greensboro. Photograph reproduced from George S. Bradshaw, comp. and ed., *The History of the First North Carolina Reunion at Greensboro, N.C.* (Greensboro: Joseph J. Stone and Co., 1905), facing 95.

During the New South era two former academies in Guilford County became degree-granting institutions, helping to make Guilford one of the educational centers of the state. New Garden Boarding School was rechartered as Guilford College in 1887. In 1905 Lucy H. Robertson, the first woman to serve as a college president in North Carolina, resuscitated Greensboro College from the effects of a disastrous fire that had occurred the previous year. The institution awarded its first degrees in 1912. In 1873 the Freedmen's Aid Society had established Bennett Seminary, a normal school, in the basement of St. Matthew's United Methodist Church in Greensboro. In 1889 the Women's Home Mission Society of the Methodist church began to support the school in a move that would have far-reaching consequences in the subsequent development of Bennett College. One student of Greensboro's history noted that the colleges located there "added a distinctive dimension" to the city's cultural life that few cities in the state enjoyed.

The immediate post-Civil War years were a time of difficulty for North Carolina's schools. The state constitution of 1868 provided for the creation of public schools but did not authorize state funding to operate them. The

Archdale Hall, built in 1885 on the campus of Guilford College, is one of the largest buildings erected in Guilford County prior to 1890 that is still in use. Photograph supplied by the author.

schools were bankrupt, and opposition to taxation and especially the education of freedmen led to stagnation. The law authorized each township in Guilford County to elect a school committee, levy taxes, erect a school, and hire a teacher. In 1872 only seven of Guilford's eighteen townships had schools in operation. The schools were generally found in log cabins, with the three Rs taught by poorly prepared teachers. When roads became impassable during bad weather, the schools were closed.

In 1885 the North Carolina General Assembly authorized the appointment of county boards of education. That year the county's magistrates and commissioners named Jesse R. Wharton county superintendent of schools and began an effort to improve conditions. Wharton succeeded in enrolling seventy-two percent of the county's eligible white children and eighty-one percent of the eligible black children. In spite of Wharton's accomplishments, the authority to set tax rates for the support of the public schools remained with the respective townships. By ruling in 1887 that levying property and poll taxes for the support of schools was not a "necessary expense" of government, the North Carolina Supreme Court effectively stymied the efforts by Wharton and others.

Guilford continued to operate its school system with a minimal tax, but in some years it was barely possible to maintain a four-month term. There was little in the way of improvements to facilities. Relief finally came after

The development of Greensboro's Bennett College in the late nineteenth century represented an important effort to educate African-American women in that era. Shown above is an early campus scene. Photograph from *1981 Bennett College Alumnae Directory* (Montgomery, Ala.: College and University Press, 1981), x.

1901 when the General Assembly, under the leadership of Governor Charles B. Aycock, appropriated money for distribution to the counties to equalize educational opportunity in the state.

In 1903 Thomas R. Foust became Guilford's county superintendent and began to modernize its school system. The most important aspects of Foust's program were a countywide tax, improved opportunities for black children, and, by 1920, the development of twenty-nine rural high schools. Foust felt a deep concern for the needs of country people and made sure that his new high schools offered courses in agriculture and domestic science. To assure access to schools in Jamestown and Pleasant Garden, the county erected dormitories and teacherages at those facilities. Foust retired in 1945, having served as a county superintendent longer than anyone else in American history.

The history of schools in Guilford is complicated. By the end of the nineteenth century three school systems began to emerge in the county. Given the fact that Guilford was a county with three separate governmental units, that was probably inevitable. As township control was eliminated, the county achieved some measure of centralization but lost control of the city schools.

Greensboro's municipal charter empowered it to create a school tax district and develop its own graded school system. With the appointment of a school board in 1890 the city moved to a new level of independence from the county. The problem in Greensboro, however, was rapid population growth, which by 1904 led to overcrowding and double shifts in most schools. Greensboro did create the first high school in the county in 1903, but not until the 1920s was the problem of overcrowding resolved temporarily with new construction. A further separation of Guilford's three systems took place in the 1920s with the creation of special charter school districts for each city.

In the late nineteenth century public health was not a major concern of local officials except in times of crisis, most often an outbreak of typhoid fever or smallpox. The diseases of childhood—diphtheria, measles, and whooping cough—were part of life's hazards. Change began to come in 1877, when the General Assembly enacted legislation creating a state board of health, as well as county boards of health comprised of all physicians in the respective counties and required all members of county medical societies to consider themselves members of their county's board of health. The question was: If the board never met, who took responsibility for public health? From this faltering start the state gradually began to provide vaccines to localities, to collect vital statistics, and to distribute educational materials.

Since the law did not require establishment of a professionally staffed county health department to practice preventive medicine, the justices of the various county courts (and later the county commissioners) were free to ignore health conditions in rural areas. Greensboro created the county's first board of health in 1905 in response to several epidemics of typhoid fever, one of which had killed thirteen students and one staff member at the State Normal School. At about the same time, High Point enacted a set of health rules and regulations.

Major concerns in both Greensboro and High Point were the elimination of rats and flies and the cleanliness of vegetables and meat in stores. Cities utilized their police to enforce existing sanitation laws, but counties, lacking a police force, made no such efforts. In 1911 the General Assembly mandated the appointment of physicians as full-time county health superintendents. In response to that legislation, Guilford's county commissioners created a county health department—the first such agency in North Carolina and the second in the United States.

For a number of years Dr. William M. Jones was the department. Jones, a hardworking resident of High Point, was constantly on the move examining and inoculating schoolchildren, checking on school sanitation, and making pictorial presentations with a magic lantern. Jones worked untiringly but never won the battle against the flies that overran the county every summer. He distributed thousands of informational pamphlets through grocery stores, joined the Rockefeller-sponsored effort to eliminate hookworm, enforced quarantines, and toward the end of his service led the successful financial campaign to construct a county tuberculosis sanitarium in Jamestown.

Another problem was the need for good housing for working-class families. As the population grew, keen competition for existing dwellings made that need more acute. For the average worker in the early twentieth century, space was at a premium. One observer noted in 1904 that "as soon as a family moves out someone rushes to the rental office to rent the house being vacated." Such demand led to speculative enterprises such as the Glenwood subdivision southwest of Greensboro, where individuals could have houses built in a wide range of prices and construction moved ahead rapidly. Some industries solved the housing problem by creating mill villages, and there were others in Guilford besides the Cones'. The Pomona mill village in Greensboro and the Highland mill village in High Point, both still partially intact, are examples. But the most effective response to the problem came in the form of groups of builders who organized to erect dozens of frame houses on the fringes of the cities. One contemporary noted that those builders made "a pot of money" but likewise acknowledged that such schemes met the need for low-income housing and did so quickly.

In Greensboro, housing for the black community moved eastward to the area around North Carolina A&T, where the black business and academic elite erected a number of substantial dwellings. One such development, known as Nocho Park, was developed by and for blacks, but many of the houses black people occupied were owned by white landlords who put them up as profit-making ventures. One black residential section, later known as the Bull Pen, became the site of a major public housing development in the 1960s. The focal point of black community life was the business district on East Market Street, which peaked in the mid-twentieth century before falling victim to urban renewal programs.

Guilford County's cities resembled other urban areas in the interior of the South as they industrialized, created transportation systems, and attracted a work force. While the creed of the New South has come in for its share of criticism, its manifestation in Guilford's cities could hardly be described in strictly negative terms. Guilford emerged as a reasonably well-balanced urban/industrial center. Its new state-supported colleges were prime examples of the emphasis on practical matters based on opportunity for individual improvement. Outside capital was a necessity for the construction of factories, but the insurance companies were locally capitalized. The civic leaders of Greensboro and High Point, apparently too concerned with the future to dwell on the past, never got around to erecting Confederate monuments at principal intersections in either town.

They did, however, devise a means for preserving the site of the Battle of Guilford Courthouse. David Schenck, who arrived in Greensboro in 1881 as an attorney for the Richmond and Danville Railroad, initiated the effort. Schenck examined the area in which the battle was fought and found little to indicate the intense struggle that had taken place there on March 15, 1781. He recorded in his diary that out of 3,000 people in Greensboro, only "half a dozen can point out the scene of the battle." In October 1886 he wrote that he was going to "save the battlefield" and soon bargained successfully for thirty acres of land.

This 1906 view of Greensboro's Elm Street, looking south, suggests that nearly a century after the committee to locate a new seat for Guilford County had completed its work, the resulting town had evolved into a grim commercial landscape unrelieved by any public space other than the streets. Photograph from the files of the Division of Archives and History.

Schenck did not have sufficient funds to buy all the land he needed, so he formed the Guilford Battleground Company, which on March 7, 1887, received a state charter to preserve the battle site and erect "monuments, tombstones, and other memorials to commemorate the heroic deeds of the American patriots who participated in this battle for liberty and independence." Schenck and his associates issued 1,000 shares of stock at $25.00 per share and were able to "redeem . . . from oblivion" more than 125 acres of land on which the battle had been fought.

David Schenck (1835-1902) inaugurated a movement to preserve the site of the Battle of Guilford Courthouse. The creation of Guilford Courthouse National Military Park was the ultimate result of Schenck's early efforts. Photograph from Bradshaw, *History of the First North Carolina Reunion*, facing 129.

In 1891 Guilford Battleground Company opened a museum on the battlefield and erected two massive granite gates to honor North Carolina Revolutionary War leaders Francis Nash and William Lee Davidson. The Cape Fear and Yadkin Valley Railroad (subsequently the Atlantic and Yadkin), whose tracks bordered the site, provided trains that brought people to Fourth of July celebrations and other patriotic events held at the battleground early in the twentieth century.

In 1895 the company opened an observation tower and initiated an effort to turn the battlefield into a historic shrine—"a repository for the remains of patriotic and distinguished individuals." As a result, two North Carolina signers of the Declaration of Independence—John Penn and William Hooper—were interred there. Within the first thirty years of its existence, Guilford Battleground Company erected twenty-seven monuments, cleared a number of grounds and trails, and attained David Schenck's goal of preservation. The park is one of the earliest efforts made to preserve a Revolutionary War site in the United States.

In 1911 Congress appropriated $30,000 to erect an equestrian monument to General Nathanael Greene. The resulting statue was dedicated on July 3, 1915. Two years later, on March 2, 1917, Guilford Battleground Company ceded the battleground to the United States government, which named it Guilford Courthouse National Military Park. In recent years citizens interested in supporting and preserving the park and its surroundings re-created the Guilford Battleground Company.

IV
1920-1960

During the prosperous twenties, the Great Depression, World War II, and the expansive postwar era, Guilford County mirrored the changes taking place in the nation while simultaneously retaining its individuality. The county's population more than tripled between 1920 and 1960. Growth was constant, and the county and its major cities created planning agencies to deal with it. Industrial expansion continued even during the Great Depression, and World War II brought economic advantages rather than disruption. After the war there was little dependence upon national defense as Guilford's economy came to achieve a healthy diversification. The quality of government and services, education, transportation, industrial development, as well as basics such as adequate housing, remained the permanent issues of Guilford's civic and economic life.

The Southern Railway's influence on Guilford was apparent by the 1920s. Since Greensboro and High Point lay on the Southern's main line, citizens could ride the new Crescent and Piedmont Limited trains, which were pulled by giant green and gold locomotives. In addition, more than twenty other passenger trains departed Greensboro in six different directions each day. Greensboro's extensive and convenient rail connections and terminal facilities became a major factor during World War II, when the United States Department of War selected the city as the site for an Army Air Forces base.

With the change to state control of the highway system in the 1920s, the county benefited from the improvements that resulted. The state constructed a concrete highway between Greensboro and High Point and dedicated it in ceremonies held in the community of Sedgefield in May 1927. The new road provided for vastly improved connections between the two cities and made it easier for residents of High Point to get to the county seat.

The state's goal was to interconnect all the county seats with paved and numbered highways. Since the routes passed through the centers of cities and towns, railroad grade crossings became a problem. In Greensboro, for instance, trains sometimes blocked streets for up to an hour. In order to

This view of the intersection of Elm and Market streets in downtown Greensboro shows the Jefferson Standard Life Insurance Company Building under construction about 1922. The structure, which dominated downtown Greensboro's skyline until the mid-1960s, is listed in the National Register of Historic Places. Photograph from the files of the Division of Archives and History.

eliminate its "Chinese Wall" of crossings, in the late 1920s Greensboro issued bonds to finance construction of underpasses.

Railroads and roads were not new, but airmail and air travel were; thus, the creation of an airport was the most significant development in transportation in the 1920s. That effort began in 1925 when Mayor E. B. Jeffress succeeded in getting Greensboro placed on a proposed U.S. airmail route. The Tri-City Airport Commission (which represented Greensboro, High Point, and Winston-Salem; the latter city withdrew from participation in the commission in 1927) established an airport eight miles west of town at a tree nursery, and in June 1927 Pitcairn Airlines began airmail service to that facility. Pitcairn subsequently became Eastern Airlines and inaugurated passenger service in December 1930 with "gigantic" eighteen-passenger Condor aircraft. Lindley Field, as the airport was first named, was the busiest airport in North Carolina for several years.

In 1937 Eastern Airlines' new DC-3s began landing on the airport's first paved runways, which were a mere 2,500 feet long. Two years later the Greensboro and High Point chambers of commerce collaborated to raise $67,000 to lengthen the runways to 4,000 feet. In 1941 the Guilford County Board of Commissioners created the Greensboro-High Point Airport Authority. That year Ceasar Cone II, son of the cofounder of Cone Mills, began his pivotal twenty-six-year tenure as secretary of the airport authority.

High Point's railway station, shown in the photograph at top as it appeared ca. 1910, remains in partial use by AMTRAK. The photo shows the dangerous grade crossings that could be deadly to motorists attempting to cross them in advance of approaching trains. Demands by Greensboro civic leaders and the needs of the traveling public led to construction of a new railroad station in downtown Greensboro in 1927. The station, no longer in use, is shown in the bottom photo (1976). Photographs from the files of the Division of Archives and History.

Guilford was on the cutting edge in transportation, but its county government—never widely known for progressive measures or attitudes—was clearly in need of change by the 1920s. The well-proportioned new $500,000 courthouse—the county's sixth—faced with Mount Airy granite, was a step forward, but it did not improve the quality of government. The building, erected in 1918, was the result of efforts begun by local lawyers and politicians in 1911 to have a courthouse "not for our generation but for our great-great grandchildren." Citizens of High Point had agreed that a new courthouse was needed but had urged that the county commissioners designate a site conveniently located somewhere between the two cities. Their advice went unheeded, and the new courthouse remained in downtown Greensboro. Many people in High Point continued to resent the inconvenience of having to travel to Greensboro to conduct county business. High Point residents received some relief in 1938 when the county

Guilford County's sixth courthouse (*right*), erected in 1918, served until the county's seventh such facility (*left*) was completed in 1973. The 1918 courthouse remains in use as the site of county offices and meeting spaces. Photograph (1978) from the files of the Division of Archives and History.

opened an administrative office there; but not until 1962 did High Point have its own courthouse and jail, making Guilford a county with courthouses located in two of its cities.

In the early part of the twentieth century North Carolina's counties came under the critical eye of proponents of scientific management. That scrutiny came mainly from those who recognized the rising efficiency of city governments, which contrasted sharply with the administration of the counties. Guilford was not immune to the haphazard, inadequate, and inefficient practices that had come to characterize county government in North Carolina. The gap between municipal and county governments grew even wider as cities began to provide services on an expanded basis and to employ professional managers and specialists. County governments existed as catchalls and gave the appearance of being detached and lackadaisical in their functions. That negative image derived in part because the commissioners were limited by law and served largely as arms of the General Assembly. Thus, their monthly meetings were not occasions for passing ordinances but were taken up with cases of people requesting exemption from taxes, admission to the county home, or other minor individual matters.

By the 1920s newspapers in Greensboro and High Point had become persistent critics of the quality of county government. That criticism contributed to the appointment in 1925 by Guilford's board of commissioners of one of the first county managers in North Carolina. (Two years later the General Assembly joined in the movement for efficiency by requiring every county to prepare a systematic budget.) In 1928 the county added a purchasing agent and an accountant, and in 1931 the commissioners completed the process of reorganization by appointing a tax collector, thus ending the archaic practice of having the sheriff perform the duty of collecting taxes.

With the Great Depression of the 1930s came the beginning of the large-scale relief and welfare programs that have remained central features of county government ever since. Budget reductions forced the temporary abandonment of the county-manager system, but Guilford remained solvent as a result of the state's takeover of school and road financing, as well

One of the largest New Deal work-relief projects in Guilford County was the lowering of the railroad tracks in downtown High Point, which put an end to the city's "Chinese walls" and the dangerous conditions that accompanied them. Photograph from McPherson, *High Pointers of High Point*, 108.

as the fact that Guilford had the highest property valuation of any county in the state. The commissioners refused to cut property taxes but did not hesitate to cut teachers' salaries and services and to issue scrip to county employees.

If the commissioners expected appreciation for guiding Guilford through the Great Depression, it was not forthcoming. The *Greensboro*

Daily News said that Guilford was the "best county"—but "not so the county government." In June 1937 the High Point Chamber of Commerce began calling for a study of county government aimed at reducing taxes and expenses. The Greensboro Chamber of Commerce, the real estate boards of both cities, and the Guilford Grange endorsed the proposal. Later that year representatives of those five organizations combined to form the Guilford County Better Government Institute to study the nature of county government.

By 1940 the pressure for greater economy and efficiency in government had risen to the point that the commissioners themselves agreed to such a study, but they refused to let the Better Government Institute look at the county's books. By again hiring a professional county manager in 1942, Guilford's commissioners alleviated to some degree the public concern over effective government, but voters, apparently piqued by what they considered a cover-up, elected an entirely new board that year.

At the end of World War II the Institute of Government at Chapel Hill conducted an extensive study of North Carolina's county government system. The study concluded that "Guilford's people are extremely fortunate" because the county had the potential to become "the leading county of the state." The report sounded good to the citizens of Guilford, but it detailed a number of concerns—among which was the long-standing need to consolidate the three health departments in the county. A growing population brought problems relating to public health, but the cities continued to go their own ways. In 1937, with support from the federal government, the High Point City Council appointed a full-time health director and a staff. Greensboro haughtily continued to insist that its department was the best in the county and that to tamper with it would be dangerous. The trend was away from municipal health departments, however, and public health was destined to come under the control of the counties in the postwar era.

Some of Guilford's leaders long had noted that public health matters did not seem to observe municipal boundaries, and as early as 1929 others had questioned the need for three health departments. The recommendations of the 1945 Institute of Government study were a beginning, but the matter remained in limbo until 1948, when Guilford County underwent the worst outbreak of poliomyelitis of any place in the United States.

The severity of that epidemic forced all the health departments in the county to work together to construct the Central Carolina Convalescent Hospital in Greensboro. That cooperation led to long-term results, and within a year the three health agencies had merged into a consolidated Department of Public Health. Although there were some complaints that the high quality of Greensboro's department was lost, the new department quickly demonstrated its competence and relieved the cities of an activity that they could no longer carry out effectively. By the early 1950s the major problems of consolidation had been resolved and Guilford's Department of Public Health had become a model.

There were other changes in the area of health. As soon as the 140-bed tuberculosis sanitarium, built in 1923, was open, it was quickly filled and had to be expanded in 1935 because of the number of cases. Even so, one of its directors, Dr. Merle D. Bonner, recalled that "Sometimes we'd have to call on eight or ten people before we found one alive to fill up a bed." During its thirty-two years of operation, the sanitarium was a major item in the county budget but was finally closed in 1955 after the introduction of new medications that allowed patients to be treated at home. Additional relief from deadly diseases came with the development of the Salk vaccine for polio, enabling the Central Carolina Convalescent Hospital to close in 1958.

The consolidation of the county's health departments was part of a long, evolutionary process that included a detailed study by a respected outside agency, a tragic polio epidemic, and pressure from the state and federal governments. Consolidation was not the case with the schools, in which the separation of county and city systems tended to become a permanent characteristic. While other populous counties in the state moved toward consolidation of their school systems, Guilford went in the opposite direction.

In 1923, as a result of the expansion of Greensboro's city limits, the question of consolidation of the county's three public school systems was put to a vote. Consolidation lost by a vote of 4,580 to 3,722. In 1927 the state chartered the greater Greensboro School District, which included a school board to be appointed by the city council. High Point created a similar district the following year. Under those arrangements county schools would be absorbed into the municipal systems as city boundaries expanded. During the Great Depression the state assumed financial responsibility for an eight-month school term for the three systems, preventing financial problems from forcing consolidation. The question of consolidation disappeared for the next five decades before being revived in the 1980s; Guilford's voters approved it in a 1991 referendum.

By the latter half of the 1920s the last vestiges of the county schools' past were being eliminated as Superintendent Thomas R. Foust worked to consolidate schools and construct modern brick buildings. In 1921 the General Assembly enacted legislation that enabled counties to submit to public referendum the question of abolishing individual school districts at the township level and instituting countywide school taxes. Following an initial defeat, proponents of change in Guilford called for another vote in 1925, which succeeded. The local referendum eliminated the county's small districts and instituted a special tax to finance an eight-month school term in the county and its cities. The referendum carried by a vote of 5,433 to 5,186. The measure also gave the three systems the option of adding a ninth month; Greensboro and High Point immediately exercised that option.

In the county system in the 1920s Foust was concerned with basics such as enforcement of compulsory attendance laws and the maintenance of a 178-day school year. By the spring of 1924 he had eliminated the last of the old one-teacher log cabin "dungeons"—a major turning point in county school history. Under Foust, Guilford led the state in the practice of busing. By the fall of 1926 seventy-one buses and thirteen automobiles were transporting pupils to and from school in the county.

Before the Great Depression the public school systems of Guilford began construction programs with emphasis on high schools. Intermunicipal rivalries added impetus to those programs. Both Asheville and Winston-Salem opened modern high schools in 1919, which left residents of Guilford with a feeling of inadequacy. High Point led off with High Point Central, which was followed by James B. Dudley High School for blacks in Greensboro. Greensboro High School (now Grimsley High) opened in 1929 after a lengthy dispute over its location, which was then beyond the built-up area of the city.

The origins of Greensboro High School lay in the opening of Dudley High. According to John A. Tarpley, principal of Dudley from 1929 to 1965, Superintendent Frederick Archer realized that anything "built for blacks would have been better than what the whites had," and Archer knew that whites "couldn't stand the thought" of black facilities' being better; so a new building for whites was mandated.

Prior to the creation of Dudley High, there was no high school for blacks in Greensboro, so college-bound youths entered preparatory programs such as the ones at Bennett College or Palmer Memorial Institute at Sedalia. Palmer was founded in 1901 by Charlotte Hawkins Brown with help from the American Missionary Society. The school opened in an abandoned blacksmith shop and by 1908 consisted of substantial buildings on 200 acres of land. For years Palmer prospered as an elite preparatory school that sent 90 percent of its graduates to college before fires, the death of Dr. Brown, and declining financial support led to its closing in 1971. At the present time the campus is a state historic site devoted to the study of the history of North Carolina's African-American citizens.

In High Point the high school for blacks was the Normal and Industrial School, which the Society of Friends (Quakers) operated with financial aid from the city. By 1923 pressures from within and without disrupted the arrangement. Normal and Industrial passed from private to public hands, and the campus was renamed Normal High School. Later in the 1920s the facility was modernized with the addition of more classrooms, an auditorium, a gymnasium, and a library. The institution's name was changed to William Penn High School; it was "reputed to be one of the most modern and completely equipped negro high schools not only in North Carolina, but in the entire South," according to the *High Point Enterprise*.

At the same time, the county system constructed a number of small high schools that were conveniently located but deficient in well-rounded programs. Superintendent Foust's major problem was bringing those schools up to state-imposed standards. With 154 students graduating from Guilford's rural high schools in 1923, the county led the state, but only Pomona, Jamestown, and Pleasant Garden high schools were accredited by the state. By 1926-1927 Gibsonville, Monticello, McLeansville, Alamance, Bessemer, Rankin, Sumner, Summerfield, and Guilford met state accreditation standards. Pomona entered the Greensboro system in 1926. So long as racial segregation was maintained, however, none of the county's black high school programs met the state's requirements.

Many felt that there needed to be an equalization of educational opportunity throughout the county. In 1926 Greensboro claimed to spend "more money per white child . . . than any other city in North Carolina." At $56.39 it was not only ahead of the county, which spent only $38.62 per white child, but also most of the South as well. It was a different story for most of the county's black schools, however. In Guilford there were still fourteen one-teacher schools out of a total of thirty-three for blacks, while there were only three one-teacher schools out of forty for whites. The students at the greatest disadvantage were in black high school programs housed in unified schools. In 1926-1927 the county's 134 black high school students received instruction from only two teachers, for a student-teacher ratio of 67 to 1. White high schools had 1,174 students and 52 teachers, for a ratio of 22.6 to 1.

With the coming of the Great Depression concern about ratios, construction, and equalization gave way to the problems of staying afloat financially. In 1933 the General Assembly shifted from paying for schools with the ad valorem property tax to a statewide sales tax of three percent, with the money to be distributed in proportion to the number of school-age children in each county. All systems were required to provide a minimum eight-month school term. Under that plan North Carolina continued to pay its teachers on time and in cash, and no schools were closed.

Nevertheless, the resulting reduction in state funding forced the Greensboro and High Point systems to go from nine-month to eight-month terms. The drop in funds also necessitated the elimination of enrichment programs such as music and library resources, which had made the city schools distinctive. The two systems reduced their teacher force, and by 1935 Greensboro's system had seventy-seven fewer teachers than in 1930. Such reductions led the Southern Association of Colleges and Secondary Schools to strip Greensboro's and High Point's high schools of their accreditation.

Fortunately, the 1933 law permitted localities to impose a tax to supplement teachers' pay; voters in Greensboro and High Point approved such a measure in May 1936. That tax, fifteen cents per $100 valuation, provided salaries for restoration of the ninth school month and helped to meet requirements for accreditation. In 1938 full accreditation was restored to both systems.

By the end of the fourth decade of the twentieth century the public school systems of Guilford County had reached a state of equilibrium. Not until the late 1950s did any major changes occur. The three separate systems remained jealous of each other's prerogatives and resisted any attempts at consolidation. The white county high schools had been brought up to state standards, and the city schools had met regional requirements. Community leaders were giving some thought and money to better educational opportunities for blacks. It was hoped that every child who should be in school would be there and that everyone who desired it could acquire a high school education.

When the Supreme Court of the United States issued its decision in *Brown v. Board of Education of Topeka* in May 1954, the Greensboro Board of Education voted six to one to instruct its superintendent to study "the ways and means for complying with the court's decision." That vote, one of the first positive reactions to the court ruling in the South, led the *Philadelphia Inquirer* to title an editorial "Greensboro shows the way." But almost immediately Superintendent Ben L. Smith ran into the restraining hand of state officialdom. Officials of the administration of Governor Luther H. Hodges ordered Greensboro not to act until the state as a whole was ready to move. In July 1957 the schools of Greensboro, Winston-Salem, and Charlotte implemented the pupil assignment law, popularly known as the "Pearsall plan." Under that law students could request reassignment and the pertinent school board would review each case individually. The Greensboro board approved six requests by blacks for transfers to white schools for the 1957-1958 school year. Five of the black pupils reported to Greensboro's Gillespie Park School on September 3, 1957, to become the first students to desegregate a public elementary school in the Southeast. The following day at Greensboro High School, Josephine Boyd became the first black student to integrate a public high school in the region. High Point began to desegregate its schools under the Pearsall plan in 1959. The county system did not begin implementing the Pearsall plan until 1964.

In higher education, the North Carolina College for Women (forerunner of UNC-Greensboro) was accredited in 1921 and began awarding its first graduate degrees in 1922. The emphasis on teacher training and home economics, enriched by requirements in the liberal arts, continued to be the essence of its instructional programs. Male students were first admitted in 1964. UNCG became an emerging university with twelve doctoral programs, numerous master's programs, and an enrollment of more than 10,000 students by the 1991-1992 academic year.

Remarkably, for a place that already had four colleges, Guilford gained a fifth institution of higher learning in 1924 when High Point College opened. The new school resulted from an intense campaign by residents of High Point to attract a college that the Methodists had decided to establish in North Carolina. High Point offered sixty acres and $100,000 in seed

Greensboro College, traditionally a school for women, began admitting male students in 1961. It is one of seven colleges and universities presently located in Guilford County. Shown here is the college's Main Building. Photograph (1976) from the files of the Division of Archives and History.

money and was selected as the site for the proposed institution. Keeping the new college going was "no easy task," according to William R. Locke, its historian, and it went into bankruptcy during the Great Depression. During World War II High Point College was host to an Army Air Forces cadet-training program, gaining new buildings and other facilities, which enabled it to prepare for the influx of student veterans in the postwar era.

Under the leadership of President Ferdinand D. Bluford, A&T went co-ed in 1928. The 1930s saw the dropping of several degree programs and the creation of a school of engineering. A&T had as its mission the teaching of "practical agriculture, the mechanic arts, and such branches of learning as relate thereto, not excluding academic and classical instruction." In 1939, the year it was accredited, A&T had graduate programs in agriculture, education, and engineering and was classified as one of four Class A colleges for blacks in the South. At the outbreak of World War II a senior Army ROTC unit was established at A&T. In 1952 an Air Force ROTC unit was established, adding to the opportunities for A&T students to find careers in military service.

A&T was elevated to university status in 1967, reflecting the growth of technology. The following year the institution's engineering school received accreditation; the university then housed the second largest computer science research center in North Carolina. At present, A&T has a nationally recognized African Heritage Center. Nevertheless, its traditional emphasis on agricultural education continues, with special attention devoted to one-on-one instruction.

Bennett College, under the presidency of David D. Jones (1926-1955), was restructured from a junior college and high school into a full four-year college. Its first college students were graduated in 1930, the year it received a "Superior" rating from the North Carolina Department of Public Instruction. The Southern Association of Colleges and Secondary Schools accredited Bennett in 1957.

Other changes in higher education included the development of the downtown campus of Guilford College, which a group of businessmen established as a night school in 1948 to make available business and technical education for veterans and other adults. Guilford College acquired the program in 1953, raised money to erect a building, and subsequently obtained the help of philanthropist Charles A. Dana in doubling the building's size.

A significant development was the creation of Guilford Technical Community College, which originated in 1958 as the Guilford Industrial Education Center. That institution, a cooperative venture of the North Carolina Department of Trade and Industrial Education and the school systems of Guilford County, was designed to provide skilled workers for new industries in the Piedmont. In 1965 it relocated at the old county tuberculosis sanitarium in Jamestown, whose abandoned hospital buildings served as classrooms and offices before being gradually replaced by modern structures.

The full impact of the Great Depression did not arrive in Guilford County until the summer of 1932. Furthermore, conditions were not as devastating in Guilford as they were in some other places because the county's basic industries included a good combination of products and purchasers. The manufacture of patent medicine picked up as people increasingly were obliged to rely more upon home remedies such as Vick's Vaporub (manufactured in Greensboro by Vick Chemical Company) and less on physicians; the need for work clothes produced by Greensboro's Blue Bell Manufacturing Company—from fabrics produced by Cone textile mills—increased as the decades wore on. The Mock, Judson, Voehringer (MOJUD) hosiery plant in Greensboro expanded three times during the Depression as women continued to demand full-fashioned silk stockings. Owners of life insurance policies sacrificed to keep up premium payments rather than allow their policies to lapse, helping to keep the Jefferson Standard and Pilot Life insurance companies solvent. Furniture and textiles, however, were under considerable stress, especially during a series of strikes in 1934, but most companies survived. Production of cigars continued as people smoked out of habit or to relieve tension.

During the Great Depression, financial institutions faced the most serious problems of all local businesses, and some banks in Greensboro and High Point were closed for as long as six months during 1933. The construction industry also was hit hard as construction of homes and commercial buildings faded away until New Deal recovery measures began to take hold. There were only a few major New Deal construction projects in Guilford County, one of which was the excavation of a deep railroad cut in High Point. The Civilian Conservation Corps worked extensively in Guilford and is remembered fondly for the recreational facilities its workers created and the trees they planted along roadsides, as well as the agency's embodiment of the work ethic, so dear to most residents of Guilford. The Works Progress Administration (WPA) put about 100 women to work in a factory on Commerce Place in downtown Greensboro, where they canned beef purchased by the government from distressed farmers in the Dust Bowl and distributed it to the needy. WPA workers constructed the boulevard portion of West Market Street in Greensboro, making that entry into the city a lasting and worthy memory of relief activities carried out during the Depression decade.

The resilience of Guilford's economy during the Great Depression is noteworthy, although it cannot be said that there was not suffering and despair for numbers of people. In general, however, most of the county's residents were able to hold their own, while some people even came from other places to find employment in Guilford's cities. When construction of four additional stories to the Southern Furniture Exposition Building in High Point began in 1939, many saw the project as an indication of improving economic conditions generally.

At the time of the nation's entry into World War II the prospect for the future of the local economy seemed less than bright to the county's business community. To some it appeared as bleak as it had been in the depths of the Great Depression. When the Japanese bombed Pearl Harbor, Guilford County had no military bases or industries that were directly connected to war-making. Conditions changed suddenly in the spring of 1942 when the Pilot Life Insurance Company made available to the Army Air Forces its buildings at Sedgefield for use as a high-level training command headquarters. The army then asked that it be allowed to occupy the Greensboro-High Point Airport and closed it to virtually all civilian traffic. The airport became a station of the Ferry Command, with several hundred men involved in the servicing and maintenance of military aircraft.

Most significant of all, and totally unexpected, the army in the fall of 1942 began construction in Greensboro of Basic Training Center #10. A total of 964 temporary buildings went up on 652 acres of land in northeastern Greensboro leased from Cone Mills by the army for the duration of the war plus one year at $1,200 per year. Beginning in March 1943 trainloads of recruits, pre-aviation cadets, and nurses began to arrive in Greensboro for four to six weeks of intensive basic training prior to being sent to specialized schools or, in the case of the nurses, being commissioned. Those men and women were intelligent, usually single, in the city for only a few weeks, and had money in their pockets. They contributed mightily to the revival of Greensboro's economy after 1942.

In 1944 Basic Training Center #10 became the principal Army Air Forces Overseas Replacement Depot (ORD) for the eastern United States. As a result, the city became the locus of even more intense activity as thousands of men were processed and entrained for points of embarkation and, eventually, the European Theater of Operations. More than 330,000 military personnel passed through Greensboro between 1942 and 1946, giving the city's citizens a sense of participation in the war—a sense of participation that had seemed unlikely when the war began. Pride in that contribution remains in Greensboro, and the section of town occupied by the army is still called ORD.

During World War II Greensboro's economy was boosted when the U.S. Army Air Forces built a sprawling training center known as Basic Training Center No. 10 in the northeastern section of the city. An aerial view of the facility is shown here. BTC-10 subsequently became the principal USAAF overseas replacement depot in the eastern United States, and a large section of northeastern Greensboro became popularly known as ORD. Photograph from slide supplied by the author.

In spite of the initial appearance of having a totally civilian focus, many industries in Guilford were called upon for contributions to the war effort and produced everything from large doors for aircraft carriers to military belt buckles. Cone Mills and Carolina Steel Corporation received Army and Navy E awards. In High Point the furniture industry converted to the needs of war, and the army requisitioned the entire Southern Furniture Exposition Building for use as a records center, retaining control of the building until 1946 and providing employment to about 100 people.

In the fall of 1946 the army decamped from Greensboro in response to pressure from local leaders, who were anxious to return to peacetime business. That decision was a rare example of an American city anxious to rid itself as quickly as possible of a large military installation after World War II. Although a few of Greensboro's leaders raised their voices in hopes of retaining the ORD, most felt that it was highly desirable to have the army depart, particularly since in its wake were hundreds of buildings, which were soon utilized for everything from emergency housing to light industry to dormitories for A&T College. The availability of those structures gave a powerful boost to the local economy in the postwar era. Once again, war had been beneficial to Guilford, although nothing could make up for the loss of 157 of the county's citizens, including Mary Webb Nicholson of the Ferry Command, who died in an air crash. She was one of the first women in North Carolina to qualify for a pilot's license. Another tragic loss came with the death of Guilford's George E. Preddy, the leading air ace in Europe at the time of his death on Christmas day, 1944. Preddy was accidentally shot down by American anti-aircraft guns.

When the army returned the airport to the Greensboro-High Point Airport Authority in August 1945, the facility was three times larger than before the war and had lighted runways for nighttime operations, as well as a modern control tower. In 1947 unrelenting efforts by Ceasar Cone II brought federal funding for a 4,500-foot runway, which was complemented by 900 acres of surrounding land acquired for the purpose of preserving the undeveloped status of areas designated for future expansion. Meanwhile, several former army buildings served as an airport terminal while plans to erect a new facility were being made.

In the postwar era the automobile and airlines brought the demise of Guilford's once-extensive rail passenger service. By 1960 only four mainline trains passed through the county, along with two to Asheville and one to Durham/Raleigh. The development of other means of transportation has diminished the role of railroads in Guilford, but rail transportation has never been supplanted. With the advent of diesel locomotives the roundhouse at Pomona was abandoned, but the yard continued to service locomotives and repair rolling stock. In line with innovative railroading practices implemented by the Southern Railway, the Pomona yard became one of that company's principal points between Washington and Atlanta for loading trailers onto flatcars. Since 1976 the former Pomona yard has served as the site of Greensboro's AMTRAK station.

In 1921, after having experimented for more than a decade with a commissioner form of government, Greensboro switched to the city manager form with an elected city council, which then selected a mayor from its membership. During most of the time before 1960 a small group of white men managed the affairs of city government in Greensboro. Those men took turns being mayor and from time to time found a black person to serve with them on the council.

High Point preceded Greensboro by adopting the city manager plan in 1915, although it differed in that municipal elections were partisan. While opponents declared that it was unnecessary to clutter up local matters with Democratic and Republican labels, High Point continues to experience partisan politics at that level. Since early in the twentieth century, High Point has had a municipal hospital; it subsequently developed city-owned transportation and utility systems. In spite of such activities the Furniture City has remained a bastion of private enterprise, including the only sales agency for Rolls-Royce automobiles in a multistate region.

By the mid-1950s Guilford's cities were solving the problems of over-crowded schools and an acute shortage of middle-class housing. Greensboro did not create a housing authority or begin construction of public housing until after World War II—programs High Point had started before the war. Both cities entered into the area of recreation during the Depression with the development of parks such as Greensboro Country Park and Blair Park in High Point. City recreation programs burgeoned in the post-Depression years but were not replicated in county government, which stuck to its essential tasks involving schools, public health, welfare, and law enforcement.

Urban sprawl began to consume open land and forests as residential developments and shopping centers went up, shifting shopping patterns away from the traditional downtown. Strip development blurred city boundaries, and the old sensation of going from one distinct place to another began to diminish. Jamestown, caught between Greensboro and High Point, felt the pressure but still managed to hold its own. Until the 1970s, much of Jamestown's revenues came from the sale of alcoholic beverages, High Point being dry until then. The population of the county was 133,010 in 1930 and had reached 246,520 in 1960. In the latter year 189,877 people, or 77 percent, lived in one of the two cities.

Many of those people worked in the traditional textile and furniture industries, which continued to dominate the economy, although a myriad of new industries had arrived. They ranged from a Western Electric plant in the old Pomona Mill building to the Hatteras Yacht factory in High Point. In late 1941 an area west of Greensboro had become the eastern terminus of an oil pipeline that originated in Louisiana. That terminus is now the huge tank farm situated near the airport. The tank farm in turn generated significant trucking business to cities throughout the region. The list of industrial operations grew, especially following construction of the interstate highway system and the resulting junction of I-85 and I-40 just south of Greensboro.

One of the most important economic activities continued to be furniture display in High Point, where the Southern Furniture Exposition Building underwent repeated expansion. After the war, even with the 1940 addition, there was not enough space to handle the demands of manufacturers. The first postwar market, which opened January 20, 1947, had a record attendance of 5,147 retail furniture buyers. By 1955 a 73,000-square-foot addition to the Main Street building had increased the display area to more than 500,000 square feet. Even so, the calls for more space were relentless, and in 1959 the 152,400-square-foot Wrenn Wing was completed and connected to

This view of the International Home Furnishings Center in downtown High Point shows the structure as it appears at present. When the building was constructed in 1921 it was only ten stories tall, but frequent expansions have made it one of the largest commercial structures in North Carolina. Photograph (1993) supplied by the author.

the original structure by a bridge. This was only the beginning of a massive expansion that followed. Dozens of other display buildings that ranged as far westward as Hickory supplemented the High Point complex.

Developments in the furniture industry led directly to continued expansion of the airport, without which there would be no furniture market. Indeed, since the 1850s Guilford's future has been closely tied to the ability of its leaders to capitalize on innovations and developments in transportation and to work them to local advantage. In 1956, hoping to enhance a spirit of cooperation among the cities that subsequently became known as the Piedmont Triad, the chambers of commerce of Greensboro, High Point, and Winston-Salem called for an entirely new airport to be built on the Guilford-Forsyth county line. The Greensboro-High Point Airport Authority ignored that proposal and instead pushed ahead with construction of longer runways, an instrument landing system, and, in 1958, a 34,000-square-foot terminal with seven gates, a restaurant, a bank, and an operations office. Ceasar Cone's single-minded determination to make Greensboro-High Point the regional airport eventually succeeded, relegating Winston-Salem's Smith Reynolds Airport to the status of a feeder terminal to the trunk line twenty-five miles away.

V
1960-1990s

Since the days of William Swaim and John Motley Morehead, the people of Guilford County have exhibited a receptive attitude toward change, although usually within conservative parameters. Guilford's citizens consistently have been more interested in waiting rather than in seeking a place on the cutting edge of change. That attitude has led to enthusiasm for railroads and industrialization, as well as to the spirited competition to host colleges for women and blacks. In most minds those were not controversial goals.

Guilford's cities have been centers for sound growth and progress, which meant that they fell in line with the New South creed of balancing industrialization and diversified agriculture with racial peace. The latter meant that segregation was the accepted and seldom questioned way of life. Like other cities of the interior, Greensboro and High Point institutionalized racial segregation even more thoroughly than did some of the older coastal cities or in the old plantation black belts. There was little of the neighborhood propinquity of blacks and whites as in Charleston or Norfolk, where residential patterns followed earlier development.

High Point's boosters liked to describe their city as a "white town," since it had a smaller percentage of blacks than many other cities in North Carolina. By the end of the first decade of the twentieth century, Greensboro had enacted a full complement of segregation ordinances, including one that prohibited black- and white-owned businesses from occupying locations in the same city block. Such ordinances helped to intensify development of the emerging black business district on East Market Street. In line with patterns of the time, Greensboro's city-owned cemeteries were segregated. As has been noted, from time to time during the 1950s a black person might be found serving on a city council—as was the case with

Greensboro's Waldo C. Faulkener in the 1950s—or as a policeman, or receiving public recognition for some achievement; but such instances were always within the limits of the color line.

There was a degree of self-satisfaction locally when Guilford's people compared themselves to residents of other places in the South. There had never been a lynching in Guilford, and visiting outsiders described its black sections as among the quietest they ever had seen. Civility was said to be at the heart of race relations in Greensboro. Well-known musicians came to nightclubs on East Market Street, where people of both races went to enjoy their performances—although blacks and whites were physically separated by ropes put up by the police. World War II brought thousands of black Army Air Forces personnel to Greensboro, but the black troops never challenged the color line.

That seemingly placid scene was changed forever on February 1, 1960, when four students from A&T College took seats at Woolworth's lunch counter on Elm Street in downtown Greensboro in an act that was to have national repercussions. Similar incidents had occurred elsewhere, but the

The Greensboro sit-ins began on February 1, 1960, and are now cited as the beginning of the end of legally mandated segregation in the South. These students at North Carolina A&T College (as the facility was then known) are shown at the lunch counter of Woolworth's five-and-dime store in downtown Greensboro after having been refused service on the previous day. Shown left to right are Joseph McNeil, Franklin McCain, Billy Smith, and Clarence Henderson. Greensboro *News & Record* photograph by Jack Moebes, Greensboro; reproduced by permission.

Greensboro "sit-ins," as they came to be known, were different in that they initiated a chain reaction that spread rapidly throughout the South. Local segregation was on its way out not only in Greensboro but everywhere else. By the end of 1960 Jesse Jackson, then a student leader at A&T, and others had formed the Student Non-Violent Coordinating Committee, which pushed for direct action to obtain civil rights immediately rather than awaiting rulings by courts. Guilford's county seat had become a place that would always be remembered for beginning the movement toward radical change. If the Battle of Guilford Courthouse was the first event of national significance to take place in Guilford, the Greensboro sit-ins was the second.

Change came to county government, too, in the 1960s, although it was of a conservative nature. In 1962 Guilford's voters elected a county board of commissioners with a Republican majority for the first time since 1928. Some observers said that anger over the food tax levied by Governor Terry Sanford's administration was at the root of the historic election. A more concrete reason was that a group of young Republicans had created a strong campaign organization to push their issues and candidates. Republicans retained control of the board until 1974 and regained it in 1988.

Was this the real politics of Guilford? It had long been said that Guilford was "Republican at heart" in political orientation. Did the 1962 election give evidence that some latent force could be rallied when there were strongly felt issues or when Democrats had become complacent and self-satisfied, as they seemed to be? In the ensuing years Republican strength continued to grow.

While politics was becoming more intense, there was a clear need for planning that extended beyond Guilford County. In 1968 the governments of Guilford and Forsyth counties, along with the city governments of Greensboro, High Point, and Winston-Salem, created the Piedmont Triad Council of Governments as a coordinating agency for Guilford, Forsyth, and Davidson counties.

The work of administering what was then the second most populous county in the state increased. Throughout the nation county government was becoming the source of funding in four areas of responsibility—social services, schools, public health, and mental health. That development required expansion of old programs and the addition of new ones. Proposals to apply for seed money from the state and federal governments to finance innovative programs were encouraged, and many were accepted. The county's budget grew accordingly. Legislation that established programs such as Medicare and Medicaid added vastly to the administrative burden of the health department and the overall cost of county government. Additional responsibilities came to include child care, dental services, and environmental concerns that seemed to expand exponentially.

Since 1979 Guilford's county government has included twenty-six separate departments, with most of its budget money devoted to the requirements of health, mental health, and social services programs—although the single largest line item has been schools. The county acquired a health building in High Point and provided for mobile units to travel to outlying destinations. In June 1974 the health department moved from several locations in Greensboro to the old Burlington Industries headquarters building on North Eugene Street. The purchase of that building came as a "windfall," in that it had plenty of space and was well suited to the department's needs. Under mandate from the state, Guilford County in 1973 created a separate department of mental health, resulting in additional demands for space and personnel. In 1991 that department acquired and renovated for its use the building in downtown Greensboro that had once housed a Sears, Roebuck store.

From time to time citizens complained that the health department had stepped beyond its traditional bounds of preventive medicine and was entering the practice of medicine. While it was true that the department served indigents—mostly babies and children who had nowhere else to turn—the provision for them was in line with the goal of a healthy community. Traditional activities such as immunization continued to be a major part of the department's work, along with expanded programs in health education. There were also two county-operated nursing homes. The food-inspection program was clearly within the purposes of a health department. A corps of inspectors administered that program by visiting dairies, grocery stores, and restaurants and supervising the installation of septic tanks. Guilford's health department became a model to which other health departments in the state dispatched interns for training.

In 1969 the North Carolina General Assembly empowered the state's county commissioners to enact local zoning ordinances; that legislation in turn enabled Guilford's commissioners to fashion one of the first rural zoning ordinances in the state. The need for planning paralleled the growth of the population and industry. In line with that growth, the commissioners extended water and sewer lines. But perhaps the most obvious move in the years after 1960 was the construction of new multimillion-dollar governmental centers. In Greensboro the construction took place in 1971 in cooperation with the city, so that a new city hall was included in the resulting complex. In 1980 Guilford County completed a public health building in High Point. Ten years later the county erected in High Point a new county building with administrative offices, courtrooms, and a state-of-the-art jail. Controversy involving cost overruns in the millions of dollars and architectural and engineering problems took some of the joy away from the new buildings.

The largest single appropriation in county budgets in recent years has been for education. In 1960 Guilford had a new school superintendent,

E. P. Pearce, Jr., who guided the county system through consolidation and desegregation. On assuming office Pearce sought to address the potential challenge to the county school system posed by the ever expanding cities and their separate school systems while at the same time attempting to respond effectively to heavy demands on the county system that resulted as new residential developments filled the countryside. In the face of that population growth, most existing county school buildings were too small to serve effectively any longer. The need for new construction was clear.

The state could offer no help in the matter and any new construction would require local initiative. After 1960 a series of successful bond proposals provided for major new projects such as Ragsdale High School in Jamestown, the county's first million-dollar facility, which was followed by the construction of modern junior and senior high schools in other areas of the county. The county imposed a special tax to fund a pay supplement for teachers—something that had never been done before.

The greatest challenge county superintendent Pearce faced was desegregation. Consolidation of its high schools enabled the county to integrate black students into the new buildings. In August 1970, following several years of intense negotiations with federal officials, the county began to "pair" elementary schools. Under the county plan, students, regardless of their race, attended kindergarten and the first two grades at one school and then completed the remaining elementary grades at another school. Those schools then fed the students into new consolidated junior and senior high schools. There was no violence; the system never came under a federal court order, and federal officials never cut off funds. John E. Batchelor, historian of the county schools, credits this state of affairs to Pearce, school board attorney John Hardy, and the determination of principals, teachers, and parents to make the plan work. By October 1970 the United States Department of Health, Education, and Welfare (HEW) declared the county in compliance with its integration guidelines—a full year before the federal courts required the Charlotte-Mecklenburg school system to begin busing children to achieve desegregated schools.

Earlier, in 1963, the Greensboro school system had adopted the so-called "freedom of choice plan." Under that arrangement all students were assigned to schools of their choice. By the fall of 1964, 500 blacks were in classes with whites at sixteen schools, as compared with thirty-five blacks at only one white school in 1962-1963. But in April 1968 a team from HEW told Greensboro city superintendent Fred Weaver that the freedom of choice plan was not producing results and merely perpetuating the racial identity of eleven predominantly black schools.

When the Supreme Court in April 1971 upheld busing in the Charlotte-Mecklenburg case, the Greensboro system began pairing elementary schools and worked out a geographic distribution of high school students. It also devised a plan to secure public cooperation. In anticipation of problems, a group of citizens formed an organization known as Concerned Citizens for Schools, and each school established an Action Council. Creation of those organizations eased tensions, but Greensboro was hard pressed to find a sufficient number of school buses to carry out the pairing program. It was only through help from state resources that the problem was addressed in time for the opening of school on August 26, 1971—which began without incident.

Other developments in the field of education included the creation of private academies and schools. United Day Care Services inaugurated Head Start programs in each of the systems, with one of the most extensive efforts, a twelve-month program, taking place in High Point. The Greensboro Board of Education created the Charles D. McIver School for trainable special-needs children enrolled in either the Greensboro or the county system. In Greensboro, the Weaver Career Education Center, characterized as a place where "meters and Mozart begin to mingle," offered specialized classes to students from throughout the system.

In 1975 High Point changed from an appointed to an elected school board—a plan adopted in Greensboro in 1979. In 1978 a state law increased the size of the county school board from five to seven members in an effort to broaden the scope of its membership. But no matter how many changes were made, or new schools built, there was always the question of consolidating Guilford's three school systems. In 1991 the voters approved consolidation. The plan, which went into effect in fall 1993, represents the culmination of a long evolution in that direction.

In the closing months of World War II the idea of a vast highway system began to appear in newspaper maps that showed a number of projected four-lane routes crisscrossing North Carolina. As the plan for a federal interstate highway system developed in the late 1950s, highway planners selected Greensboro as the point at which proposed Interstates 85 and 40 would join each other. Although engineering problems resulted in dangerous intersections near the point at which the two highways met and caused the stretch of roadway to be dubbed "death valley," once again Greensboro found itself fortuitously located at a major interchange point. In 1991 the "Carolinian," an AMTRAK train, made its initial daily runs between Raleigh and Charlotte in the hope that it would attract business travelers and take some of the pressure off the highways. Even so, plans were being developed to construct a new I-85/I-40 bypass south of Greensboro.

In 1961 Ceasar Cone II, the man who said the airport was his avocation, told a reporter from the *Winston-Salem Sentinel* that Winston-Salem's name would be on the airport in Guilford "whether they liked it or not." Cone saw the development of a well-served airport as an economic necessity. In his mind the location at Lindley Field was the only logical place for a regional airport. He personally financed an appeal to the Civil Aeronau-

Ceasar Cone II served for twenty-six years as secretary of the Greensboro-High Point Airport Authority, obtaining federal funds to assist in its development and ensuring that the facility remained in Guilford County. Photograph from *Saluting Piedmont Triad International Airport*, commemorative fiftieth anniversary publication (N.p.: Piedmont Triad Airport Authority, [1991]), 19; reproduced by permission.

tics Board to so designate the field. By that time Winston-Salem's Smith Reynolds Airport was in decline, even though it was the headquarters of Piedmont Airlines, a regional carrier. Cone realized that with regional status, improvements such as the construction of fire and rescue facilities and the appointment of an executive director would be made. In March 1968, the first year of jet passenger service, the Greensboro-High Point Airport Authority adopted a $63 million master plan and implemented it during the ensuing fourteen years. Improvements came at a rapid pace. They included an 8,200-foot runway in 1970—the longest in the state at that time—and a new weather facility in 1974. In 1982 the airport authority opened a new terminal and extended the runways to 10,000 feet. The authority made peace with Winston-Salem and Forsyth County in 1985 by allowing each jurisdiction to appoint one person to serve as a member of that body. The airport authority changed the facility's name to Piedmont Triad International Airport in 1987.

Urban renewal in the 1960s and 1970s helped to eliminate some of Greensboro's and High Point's worst housing. The "Bull Pen" on the eastern side of Greensboro gave way to the Cumberland Housing Project. During the rebuilding of Warnersville, local churches supplemented public efforts at urban renewal. But no matter how many housing units were constructed, the housing authorities of Greensboro and High Point remained hard pressed to meet the demands placed on them. As older buildings deteriorated and were condemned, housing officials attempted to construct new houses on the land or in some cases to renovate the older structures. Problems with crime, drugs, and violence plague the public-housing areas of both cities in spite of heavy police presence.

Predominantly black Morningside Homes in Greensboro became the site of a shootout on November 3, 1979, when five members of the Communist

The Piedmont Triad International Airport opened the terminal complex shown at top in 1981. The massive terminal building, comprising more than a quarter-million square feet, is the largest construction project ever undertaken in Guilford County. Photograph from *Saluting Piedmont Triad International Airport*, 26; reproduced by permission.

Workers party (CWP) were shot and killed during a confrontation with members of the Ku Klux Klan (KKK). Members of the CWP termed the shootings a "massacre," but others placed the blame on both sides, inasmuch as the participants were outsiders who had chosen Greensboro as the site of the confrontation. Similar situations had occurred the previous April in Winston-Salem and the previous July at China Grove, but without gunfire.

Prior to November 3 a Communist leaflet campaign had raised the level of rhetoric in the direction of violence. The leaflet described members of the KKK as "a bunch of two-bit cowards" and challenged members of the Klan to attend a "Death to the Klan" rally to be held in Greensboro. On November 3 the Greensboro Police Department assigned only four officers to the march in the hope that a "low profile" would help avert trouble. A parade was scheduled to start at noon, but the shooting began at 11:23 A.M.— before the police arrived. The press, however, was present with television cameras in place, providing a vivid record of the violent encounter, which subsequently was televised nationally. Events transpired so rapidly that essential messages did not reach police officers promptly, but within minutes of the violence the police had arrested suspects in the shootings.

In the aftermath the police came in for heavy criticism. There was an instant reaction from the national media, which rushed representatives to Greensboro and placed heavy blame on the city's government and especially its police force. One newsman observed that "everything is race." Such hasty assessments tended to inflame passions as city officials began a comprehensive examination of race relations in the city. A report issued by a Citizens Review Committee and submitted to the North Carolina Advisory Committee to the U.S. Commission on Civil Rights faulted the police for their intelligence gathering and incorrect assumptions, especially the idea that trouble would come at the conclusion of the scheduled parade rather than before it began. A police summary indicated that no one, including members of the CWP, had expected the use of deadly force.

Jury trials of fourteen persons charged with taking part in, or conspiring to perpetrate, the incident failed to produce any convictions. A subsequent civil suit against the city of Greensboro by members of the CWP led to a decision against the city on charges that included failure to provide adequate protection at the march.

On the positive side was the perception that Greensboro had become more aware of the problems of its black community. Citizens organized a number of groups to discuss human-relations issues. As a means of improving race relations, those groups proposed a number of measures, including one that urged greater police presence at confrontational events to ensure the safety of citizens.

Entering the last third of the twentieth century, more and more women were joining the work force at all levels and becoming visible politically. Life-styles were changing for both sexes, and a fuller use of leisure time and the opportunity to spend more of it with family members began to have an ever higher priority for many residents.

By 1980 Greensboro was home to three Fortune 500 manufacturing companies—Cone Mills, Blue Bell, and Burlington Industries. All had local origins and were well respected nationally in the business community. Greensboro owed its industrialization to Cone Mills. Blue Bell had made work clothes in the city since 1912, while Burlington Industries had been in town since 1935 and had erected a new headquarters building in the northwestern part of the city. Downtown Greensboro contained the home offices of Southern Life and Jefferson-Pilot life insurance companies, both among the top thirty in the nation.

That the top ten furniture manufacturers in the Triad area employed nearly 16,000 workers in 1992 highlighted the central importance of the furniture industry. High Point was the home of Masco Home Furnishings, the largest furniture manufacturer in the world, with 5,300 employees. The furniture companies developed new lines as they continued their national domination of design and manufacturing.

This late-summer 1993 view of Greensboro's Elm Street, looking north, shows the 1991 annex to the Jefferson-Pilot building, with its towering sloped peak. The annex enabled the renowned insurance company to consolidate all of its operations in the Gate City's central business district. Photograph supplied by the author.

Other important industries located in Guilford included Twining, a tea processor that selected Guilford for its clean air; telecommunications giant AT&T; Konica, a manufacturer of cameras; Volvo-White, an international manufacturer of trucks; and TIMCO, which repairs and converts jetliners. Corporate activity multiplied the need for hospitality, transportation, and governmental services—all of which grew to accommodate it. Of central importance in the economy was the variety of industrial activity in Guilford. There was no dependence upon any single industry, and the only local natural resources being used were clay, trees, and stone. Bricks are manufactured in Pleasant Garden, and red cedar trees are processed into boards and cedar oil in Greensboro.

All seemed well until the 1980s, when some of Guilford's big names either disappeared or shrunk in size. Blue Bell and Southern Life were merged into other firms in corporate buyouts. Burlington Industries and Cone Mills went private in the face of attempted hostile takeovers, which diminished their preeminent positions. Foreign competition forced both firms to reduce operations. But if the giants had been felled, some smaller textile operations thrived, among them Texfi, Unifi, and Guilford Mills— the latter becoming the nation's leading producer of warp knit fabrics.

Another ingredient in the local economic mix was the Greensboro Coliseum, which, when it opened in 1959, was one of the largest arenas in the Southeast. For a number of years the Atlantic Coast Conference basketball

The Greensboro Coliseum is presently undergoing a second major expansion to increase its seating capacity to more than 23,000 people. The expansion will maintain the facility's ability to participate in North Carolina's competitive entertainment market. Photograph (September 1993) supplied by the author.

playoffs were a standard event in Greensboro, but when Charlotte and other cities opened coliseums Greensboro lost its dominance. Renovation and expansion of the coliseum complex began in 1991.

Large-scale development continued to come in the furniture-display activity of High Point. The need for space was relentless, and in 1967 the Green Drive Annex added 375,670 square feet to the Southern Furniture Exposition Building. That expansion brought total exhibit space to twenty-seven acres. In 1974 the mammoth Commerce Wing was completed. Between 1983 and 1985 the Design Center went up; the Hamilton Wing followed in 1990. Completion of the Hamilton Wing brought to 2.8 million square feet the total amount of display space in High Point alone. The complex, known as the International Home Furnishings Center (IHFC) since 1988, is the largest of its type in the world. In the spring of 1992 the market contained the products of 1,800 manufacturers, whose displays attracted 60,000 visitors from every state and sixty-five countries. The visitors occupied 12,000 hotel rooms, rented 1,000 homes, and spent $198 million in a process that takes place twice a year. The furniture companies remain busy in the early 1990s in spite of recessionary forces in the general economy.

The IHFC is the opposite of a tourist attraction inasmuch as admission is strictly limited to persons holding passes. Over the years the complaint has arisen that High Point is a place "where there ain't nothing to do" and that the market should be moved to a larger place. But High Point is where the

In this contemporary aerial view of High Point can be seen the size and complexity of the International Home Furnishings Center. Photograph from slide supplied by the author.

furniture is, and residents of the city reply that their city offers a "rare combination of industrial sophistication and small-town hospitality." Also in High Point is the world's largest library devoted to the history and design of furniture and the largest still-photography studio in the world.

As of early 1993 Guilford was the leading manufacturing county in North Carolina. The county stands third in population (behind Mecklenburg and Wake), but it is the only North Carolina county to contain two of the largest cities in the state. It remains an educational center with its five colleges and three universities—High Point College having become a university in 1991. Those institutions contribute heavily to the county's economy. The county remains a transportation center for rail, highway, and air traffic; and with the IHFC in High Point, Guilford's influence reaches far beyond its boundaries. With its mixed economy, it remains less vulnerable to the forces of recession than many other places.

High Point University, affiliated with the Methodist church, is one of the few institutions of higher learning in North Carolina to have received financial support from a municipality. Finch Hall (left) dominates this view of the campus. Shown at right is the university chapel. Photograph (1975) from the files of the Division of Archives and History.

If some in Greensboro or High Point claimed for their city world-class status, there were also small towns that continued to retain their identity and a flavor of their past. Gibsonville in the east, Stokesdale in the northwest, and Jamestown, which lies between Greensboro and High Point, are among a long list of such places whose very existence have been threatened by urban sprawl. Jamestown in particular was under pressure from two directions but maintained its separate identity. The presence there of a corrugated-box factory might come as a surprise, but manufacturing is nothing new in Jamestown, where the past is kept alive through the Historic Jamestown Foundation, headquartered at the old Richard Mendenhall plantation.

Stokesdale, far enough away from Greensboro to escape some of the pressure, successfully incorporated as a municipality and in 1991 elected its own town officials to avoid the prospect of being absorbed by the Gate City. Gibsonville, a mill town, suffers from the closing of Cone Mills' Minneola plant and is under economic stress, although some people who work in Greensboro find its quiet appealing. Under the most intense pressure from urban sprawl are Summerfield and Oak Ridge, where development of upscale housing is consuming the open land and farms that once characterized rural Guilford.

Development had become so intense that it became necessary to apply stringent rules to prevent construction on Greensboro's and High Point's watersheds. Thus, if Guilford overcame problems arising from the absence of waterways, the need for water itself remains a problem. The U.S. Army Corps of Engineers recently approved plans to obtain water from the Deep River by erecting a dam in Randolph County—much to the distress of people who reside near the projected facility. Other plans to obtain additional water for Greensboro are pending.

In the county's rural areas farming as a primary occupation has virtually ended, a process that began early in the century. Recently a county extension agent observed that he could think of only a few people engaged in farming in the county who did not also have some other type of work. People who work the soil still produce tobacco, grains, and soybeans, and a diminishing number operate dairy farms. A limited amount of logging takes place in some portions of the county—some of it connected with the clearing of land for development.

For some there is a sense of nostalgia about the loss of older ways of life and for simpler and more congenial times. Citizens have formed organizations to preserve artifacts, neighborhoods, and streetscapes. Greensboro created Tannenbaum Park next to Guilford Courthouse National Military Park, with hands-on and living history programs aimed at depicting life in Guilford in the eighteenth century. One major achievement in historic preservation is Blandwood, John Motley Morehead's Tuscan-style villa built in Greensboro in the 1840s. A small but determined group saved the dwelling from becoming a parking lot and subsequently established the Greensboro Preservation Society. The designation of historic districts in Greensboro and High Point led some people to purchase older houses and to renovate and restore neighborhoods that were falling into decline. Such was the case in the College Hill and Summit Avenue neighborhoods of Greensboro; in High Point preservationists worked to have certain portions of the city lying adjacent to Main Street designated as historic districts. A number of structures have been listed on the National Register of Historic Places.

There is no shortage of things to do in Guilford. In addition to the cultural life and programs provided by the colleges and universities, other activities—some supported with public money, others through private

Blandwood was completed in 1850 as Greensboro industrialist John Motley Morehead's Tuscan-style dwelling. The Greensboro Preservation Society prevented Blandwood from being demolished in the 1960s and presently maintains the stately structure as a historic site. Photograph (1970) from the files of the Division of Archives and History.

donations—are available. Guilford Courthouse National Military Park was expanded and had received a new visitors center in time for the American Revolution bicentennial in 1976; President Gerald R. Ford dedicated the new facility.

Adjacent to the battleground is the Natural Science Center, and the historical museums of Greensboro and High Point are among the best in the state. Greensboro is well provided with parks beyond its city limits, with Hagan-Stone Park in the southern part of the county and Bryan Park—a gift of the Greensboro philanthropists Joseph M. and Kathleen Price Bryan—in the northeast. Nature trails and bicycle paths have been constructed around lakes and along streams in the city. In High Point, City Lake Park once boasted one of the largest swimming pools in the South; powerboat races take place at Oak Hollow Lake, which was developed as a recreation area; and the Piedmont Environmental Center offers trails and educational programs.

In the late 1980s bond issues enabled Greensboro to expand its museums and to consolidate many of the city's cultural activities by renovating and adding to the building that previously housed the *Greensboro Daily News*, forerunner of the *News & Record*. North Carolina A&T State University developed one of the most significant African culture centers in the nation, and UNCG moved its Witherspoon Gallery of Art into a new building.

Near the front entrance to R. E. McNair Engineering Hall at North Carolina A&T State University can be seen a mounted bust of Dr. Ronald E. McNair, "astronaut, scientist, humanitarian," who died in the 1986 explosion of the Challenger spacecraft. Photograph (1993) supplied by the author.

Guilford College added an art gallery and collection when it renovated its library, and an art gallery is connected to the High Point Theater, headquarters for the annual High Point Shakespeare Festival. In the competition for cultural leadership in North Carolina, Guilford County is not lacking. There is a Greensboro Symphony Orchestra; the Greensboro Ballet; and the famous Eastern Music Festival, held every summer, which draws professionals and students from throughout the nation.

In the realm of sports, professional baseball, ice hockey, and basketball games can fill an evening, or one could attend a myriad of athletic events at local colleges and universities. The Kmart Greater Greensboro Open golf tournament continues to attract thousands every spring, as it has since 1938, with the exception of three years during World War II.

Anyone driving through the downtown sections of Greensboro or High Point after an absence of a decade would find the skylines of those cities markedly changed. After a lull in the 1970s, in which the downtowns went into decline, construction began anew with three new towers in Greensboro and several in High Point. High Point's additions include a modernistic new hospital, along with the Market Square development on West High Avenue. A number of smaller, individually owned buildings added to the space available for furniture displays. Many of those buildings feature modern designs that give downtown High Point a more sophisticated appearance. Both downtowns have new hotels, but prospects for additional development in the early 1990s seemed dimmed by the economic stresses of the times and overconstruction of office space.

VI
Conclusion

The process of dividing North Carolina into counties took place over a span of 280 years—from 1663 to 1943. Guilford County was created in 1771—near the midpoint of that period. At that time it was a mere wilderness under the administration of the British authorities—no different from the counties that surrounded it or subsequently were carved from it. The simple agricultural society of that time prevailed in Guilford during the ensuing three-quarters of a century, until the advent of the railroad began the inevitable process of modernization in the mid-nineteenth century.

During its 250 years of settlement the county has contributed only two governors to the state, most recently John Motley Morehead in the early 1840s. A relatively few other people from Guilford have attained positions of high responsibility in the state, even though Guilford has long been one of North Carolina's most populous counties. The people of Guilford were not indifferent or lacking in talent. If political scientist V. O. Key's concept of a "progressive plutocracy" of powerful businessmen controlling events is correct, it would suggest that some people in Guilford exercised political power behind the scenes. Some local citizens attribute Guilford's relative lack of influence in state government to the fact that the county's politicians have been too hard at work to take the time to build political alliances and networks or to sit in Raleigh long enough to gain seniority—strategies that lead to high positions. In the twentieth century virtually everyone from Guilford who has sought statewide office has almost uniformly failed to attain it. A notable exception is Henry Frye, an associate justice of the North Carolina Supreme Court.

In late 1992 Governor-elect James B. Hunt, Jr., began naming residents of Guilford to his cabinet—C. Robin Britt as secretary of Human Resources; Katie G. Dorsett as secretary of the Department of Administration; and S. Davis Phillips as secretary of Commerce. In doing so, the governor tapped into the pool of talented and experienced people whose work had contributed to the social, political, and industrial maturation of the county.

It has been to Guilford itself that the county's people have directed their main attention and interests. The county has experienced a slow but steady increase in population since its name first appeared on a map—an increase

The election of Henry Frye as a member of the North Carolina House of Representatives in 1968 made him the first African American to be elected to the North Carolina General Assembly in the twentieth century. Frye became an associate justice of the North Carolina Supreme Court in 1983. Photograph courtesy News & Observer Publishing Company, Raleigh; reproduced by permission.

that persisted even when the state appeared to be lagging in growth. Most of the county's people were American born, if not North Carolina born. Guilford itself probably typified the early twentieth-century claim that North Carolina was the "purest Anglo-Saxon state in the world"—the theme of a speech made by the British ambassador during a visit to Greensboro in 1905. Whatever that meant, it ignored the presence of African Americans, who have consistently comprised about 25 percent of the county's total population. In recent decades Guilford's cities have welcomed newcomers from many parts of the world, but the foreign born still represent only a very small percentage of the total population.

While the original calling of most citizens of Guilford County was agriculture, a relatively few remain on the land. High-tech farming such as computerized dairying is holding its own, but vast segments of the old farmland have been consumed by unstinting development, which continues to devour it. Resentments farmers might harbor over the loss of their land are seldom heard, although from time to time a nostalgic item about an earlier Guilford will appear in the newspapers. One has only to take a short drive in any direction to see the abandoned silos of an old dairy farm surrounded by housing or commercial structures. Fields that once produced a bounty of crops are no longer even discernible in the carefully landscaped executive centers and housing developments that have spread across them. A survey of historically significant structures in the county published in 1979 revealed a rich architectural heritage, but many of those structures have since disappeared or are under threat from development. Preservation has been primarily an urban activity with emphasis on designating as historic districts entire neighborhoods—although many individual structures have been saved from destruction. Even so, the lingering reminders of the past continue to disappear from the countryside.

One thing that remains as important at present as it did in the past, although it has changed radically, is transportation. Nothing in the past equaled the completion of the North Carolina Railroad in 1856 as a catalyst for change. It was a citizen of Guilford, John Motley Morehead, who led the program to build the railroad—and who made sure that its route passed through his hometown of Greensboro. Geography undoubtedly played a part in the selection of the route, but the line could easily have missed Guilford entirely if a slightly more southeasterly course had been chosen. Without the tracks, Guilford would have remained in isolation, perhaps for many years. But with the North Carolina Railroad in place, a different future was assured. That future was reinforced less than ten years later when the Civil War gave Guilford a rail connection to the north, which released the railroad from control by shortsighted North Carolinians who apparently refused to raise their vision beyond the state's borders.

Shown arriving at Greensboro's AMTRAK station on the morning of September 10, 1993, is the northward-bound "Carolinian." Rail passenger service has been a constant feature of Guilford County life since January 1856. Photograph supplied by the author.

From the regime of the railways through the coming of highways to the jet age, the people of Guilford have consistently recognized the desirability of convenient transportation facilities and have given such facilities the time and attention required to make sure they would be adequate to the county's needs. Such attention has persisted to the present in the form of a recent effort to obtain for the Piedmont Triad International Airport a proposed North Carolina international air cargo facility. The attempt failed, but not from want of trying.

The arrival in Guilford of various forms of transportation consistently bolstered industrialization and commercial activity there. At the end of the nineteenth century, industry arrived in full force with the development of the furniture industry in High Point and the creation of giant textile mills on the fringes of Greensboro. Earlier in the nineteenth century the attitude of Guilford's civic leaders, who welcomed commerce and development, set the stage for the industrialization that followed.

Ancillary to the new factories were the mill villages. Critics have characterized those enclaves as paternalistic and therefore detrimental to those who lived in them, but one has only to drive through old areas with their still well-maintained and well-spaced houses and yards to form a picture of a life that could not have been too bad and was certainly superior to alternatives that included subsistence tenant farming and slum tenements.

Along with the transportation facilities and industrial enterprises that developed in Guilford in the nineteenth century came urbanization. In the realm of urbanization can be found vast differences between Guilford and its neighbors. Guilford is the only county in North Carolina—and one of only a few in the nation—to have two large cities within its boundaries, a fact that seriously complicates the work of the historian. Historians also must take into account the spirited rivalries that existed between Greensboro and High Point during their early years, as well as the considerable differences between the two cities. Many North Carolinians are unaware of Guilford's complexity and tend to assume that a place of High Point's size and renown surely must be a county seat in its own right. Should they visit the Furniture City they would find a complete set of county administrative buildings, including a high-rise courthouse larger than many in the state.

Closely connected with urbanization and industrialization are commercial and service activities, beginning with insurance companies in the early

The two large buildings shown above comprise High Point's county governmental complex. At center is a public health center erected in 1985; at right is a detention center and courthouse completed in 1990. Guilford is one of only a few counties in the nation to maintain two courthouses. Photograph (September 1993) supplied by the author.

part of the twentieth century. Banks subsequently developed in Guilford, but in the modern era of consolidations and mergers, the cities of Guilford still remain among the larger places in North Carolina without the headquarters of a major bank. Similar developments in recent years resulted in the departure of one insurance-company headquarters and the consolidation of another, with the concentration of its offices in downtown Greensboro, where a new high-rise building complements the Jefferson-Pilot building, the city's original skyscraper. Some corporate headquarters have disappeared through mergers and buyouts, but the resilience of those that remain suggests that they will continue to exist.

Schools developed early, giving the county its long claim to educational leadership. There is evidence that there were leaders in Guilford whose thinking about the educational problems and needs of the state was considerably ahead of their times. Education is a central feature in any county's history, but in Guilford the picture is complicated by the long-term development of three separate and distinct school systems, each with its own traditions and claims to distinctiveness. As a result of a recent referendum, those systems are being consolidated into a single countywide unit. Nothing about school consolidation occurred without controversy, but the merging of the systems follows a trend toward increased efficiency and cost savings.

The mixture of private and public institutions of higher learning gives rich texture to the history of education in the county. No other North Carolina county has as many colleges and universities as Guilford. Its private colleges have evolved from small denominational institutions to more significant and well-balanced centers of higher learning.

In most local histories and even in historical museums, it is customary to emphasize war. It seems undeniable that Guilford has tended to share a peculiar relationship with war. One does not need to leave its borders to see the effects of war or the ways in which its people participated in war. It is a fact that the county has been a beneficiary of war to an unusual extent. While the Battle of Guilford Courthouse lasted only about two hours, the battlefield is one of the county's treasures. The Civil War and World War I gave Greensboro improvements in its rail connections and facilities that would have been longer in coming—if they would have come at all—in the absence of the conflicts. During World War II Greensboro's leaders were able to obtain for the city a military base, which gave it an economic boost. But once the war was over, Greensboro's leaders asked the military to leave as soon as possible. Guilford County and its cities then returned to the stability offered by local initiatives in industry and commerce.

These are the main themes of Guilford County's history. They represent merely a beginning of the subject, since even very small places possess a variety of historical topics that always exceed the expectations of anyone venturing into a study.

Appendix

Population of Guilford County, Greensboro, and High Point, by Year

Year	Guilford County	Greensboro	High Point
1790	7,191		
1800	9,442		
1810	11,420		
1820	14,511		
1830	18,737		
1840	19,175		
1850	19,754		
1860	20,056		
1870	21,736	2,200 (approx.; for village only)	550 (approx.)
1880	23,585	2,105 (4,497 for two townships)	991 for village only; 2,060 for township
1890	28,052	3,317	3,481 for township; village not listed
1900	39,074	10,035	4,163 (village)
1910	60,497	15,895	9,525
1920	79,272	19,861	14,302
1930	133,010	53,569	36,745
1940	153,916	59,319	38,495
1950	191,057	74,389	39,973
1960	246,520	123,334	62,063
1970	288,590	152,252	63,204
1980	317,154	155,642	63,380
1990	347,420	183,521	69,496

Suggested Readings

Albright, James W. *Greensboro, 1808-1904: Facts, Figures, Traditions, and Reminiscences.* Greensboro: Jos. J. Stone, 1904.

Arnett, Ethel Stephens. *David Caldwell.* Greensboro: Media, Inc., 1976.

_____. *Greensboro, North Carolina: The County Seat of Guilford.* Chapel Hill: University of North Carolina Press, 1955.

_____. *The Saura and Keyauwee in the Land that Became Guilford, Randolph and Rockingham.* Greensboro: Media, Inc., 1975.

_____. *William Swaim, Fighting Editor: The Story of O. Henry's Grandfather.* Greensboro: Piedmont Press, 1963.

Auman, William T. "Neighbor against Neighbor: The Inner Civil War in the Randolph County Area of Confederate North Carolina." *North Carolina Historical Review* 61 (January 1984): 59-92.

Bagwell, William. *School Desegregation in the Carolinas: Two Case Studies.* Columbia: University of South Carolina Press, 1972.

Batchelor, John E. *The Guilford County Schools: A History.* Winston-Salem: John F. Blair, 1991.

Billings, Dwight B., Jr. *Planters and the Making of a "New South": Class, Politics, and Development in North Carolina, 1865-1900.* Chapel Hill: University of North Carolina Press, 1979.

Bowles, Elizabeth Ann. *A Good Beginning: The First Four Decades of the University of North Carolina at Greensboro.* Chapel Hill: University of North Carolina Press, 1967.

Caldwell, Bettie D. *Founders and Builders of Greensboro, 1808-1908.* Greensboro: Jos. J. Stone, 1925.

Carroll, Karen W. "Sterling, Campbell, and Albright: Textbook Publishers, 1861-1865." *North Carolina Historical Review* 63 (April 1986): 169-198.

Chafe, William H. *Civilities and Civil Rights: Greensboro, North Carolina, and the Black Struggle for Freedom.* New York: Oxford University Press, 1980.

Clay, James W., et al. *North Carolina Atlas: Portrait of a Changing Southern State.* Chapel Hill: University of North Carolina Press, 1975.

Edmunds, Mary Lewis Rucker. *Governor Morehead's Blandwood and the Family Who Lived There.* Greensboro: Greensboro Printing Co., 1976; Greensboro: the author, 1987.

Gibbs, Warmoth T. *The History of North Carolina Agricultural and Technical College, Greensboro, North Carolina.* Dubuque, Iowa: Wm. C. Brown Book Co., 1966.

Gilbert, Dorothy L. *Guilford: A Quaker College.* Greensboro: Jos. J. Stone, 1937.

Hayes, Charles R., and D. Gordon Bennett, eds. *Guilford County Atlas.* Greensboro: Guilford County Board of Commissioners, 1976.

Hendricks, Howard O. "Imperiled City: The Movements of the Union and Confederate Armies toward Greensboro in the Closing Days of the Civil War in North Carolina" (master's thesis, University of North Carolina at Greensboro, 1987).

Jones, Abe D., Jr. *Greensboro 27*. Bassett, Va.: Bassett Printing Co., 1976.

Jordan, Paula S. *Women of Guilford County, North Carolina: A Study of Women's Contributions, 1740-1979*. Greensboro: Greensboro Printing Co., 1979.

Kipp, Samuel M., III. "Old Notables and Newcomers: The Economic and Political Elite of Greensboro, North Carolina, 1880-1920." *Journal of Southern History* 43 (August 1977): 373-394.

Lathrop, Virginia T. *Educate a Woman: Fifty Years of Life at the Woman's College of the University of North Carolina*. Chapel Hill: University of North Carolina Press, 1942.

Lefler, Hugh T., and Albert Ray Newsome. *North Carolina: The History of a Southern State*, 3d ed. Chapel Hill: University of North Carolina Press, 1973.

Locke, William R. *No Easy Task: The First Fifty Years of High Point College*. High Point: High Point College, 1975.

McPherson, Holt. *High Pointers of High Point*. High Point: High Point Chamber of Commerce, 1976.

Marteena, Constance H. *The Lengthening Shadow of a Woman: A Biography of Charlotte Hawkins Brown*. Hicksville, N.Y.: Exposition Press, 1977.

Murdock, Thomas G. "The Geology and Mineral Resources of Guilford County." Information Circular No. 5. Raleigh: North Carolina Department of Conservation and Development, 1947.

O'Brien, Gail Williams. *The Legal Fraternity and the Making of a New South Community: 1848-1882*. Athens: University of Georgia Press, 1986.

O'Keefe, Patrick. *Greensboro: A Pictorial History*. Norfolk: Donning Co., 1977.

Olsen, Otto H. *Carpetbagger's Crusade: The Life of Albion Winegar Tourgée*. Baltimore: John Hopkins University Press, 1965.

Pomeroy, Kenneth B. *North Carolina Lands: Ownership, Use, and Management of Forest and Related Lands*. Washington, D.C.: American Forestry Association, 1964.

Powell, William S. *North Carolina through Four Centuries*. Chapel Hill: University of North Carolina Press, 1989.

Robinson, Blackwell P., and Alexander R. Stoesen. *History of Guilford County*. Greensboro: Guilford County American Revolution Bicentennial Commission, 1981.

Smith, H. McKelden, ed. *Architectural Resources: An Inventory of Historic Architecture: High Point, Jamestown, Gibsonville, Guilford County*. Raleigh: North Carolina Department of Cultural Resources, Division of Archives and History, 1979.

Stockard, Sallie W. *History of Guilford County*. Knoxville, Tenn.: Gaut-Ogden Printers, 1902.

Stoesen, Alexander R. *Guilford College: On the Strength of 150 Years*. Greensboro: Trustees of Guilford College, 1987.

——————————. "Public Health in Guilford County," in *The History of Medicine in Greensboro, North Carolina, during the 19th and 20th Centuries: A Series of Essays by Prominent Health Care Providers*, ed. Robert L. Phillips, 2 vols. Raleigh: Printworks, 1991. (Sponsored by the Greensboro Medical Historical Library and the Medical Library of Moses H. Cone Memorial Hospital.)

Trelease, Allen W. *The North Carolina Railroad and the Modernization of North Carolina*. Chapel Hill: University of North Carolina Press, 1990.

•

Turrentine, Samuel Bryant. *A Romance of Education: A Narrative Including Recollections and Other Facts Connected with Greensboro College.* Greensboro: Piedmont Press, 1946.

United States Department of Agriculture: Soil Conservation Service. *Soil Survey of Guilford County, North Carolina.* 1977.

Warner, Stafford Allen. *Yardley Warner, the Freedman's Friend: His Life and Times with His Journal and Letters Reproduced in an Appendix.* Didcot, Pa.: Wessex Press, 1957.

Weatherly, A. Earl. *The First Hundred Years of Historic Guilford, 1771-1871.* Greensboro: Greensboro Printing Co., 1972.

Wheaton, Elizabeth. *Codename Greenkill: The 1979 Greensboro Killings.* Athens: University of Georgia Press, 1987.

Wolff, Miles. *Lunch at the Five and Ten: The Greensboro Sit-Ins. A Contemporary History.* New York: Stein and Day, 1970.

Yearns, W. Buck, and John G. Barrett. *North Carolina Civil War Documentary.* Chapel Hill: University of North Carolina Press, 1980.

INDEX